THE LIFEBOAT INN

THE MANOR HOUSE

THORNHAM

CHURCH STREET

THE HARBOUR

Thornham
then and now

John Warham
Old photographs collected by Stephen Greef

To Colin, Ian and Stephanie

▲ The new Village Hall opened its doors for
the first time on September 23rd 2013.

Contents

Introduction

In 2006, I worked with Peter Oliver and Pat Thompson to produce *Thornham, a Photographic Portrait of a Norfolk Village*, which traced the story of the village through the twentieth century. The recollections of the villagers were pulled together by Peter Oliver and illustrated with old photographs, many of which were kindly lent by people of Thornham.

This was followed in 2009 by *Thornham – People and Places*, which became the first of a mini-series of books on the North Norfolk coastal villages. *Thornham – People and Places* showed the village of the first decade of the new Millennium, through photographs of the landmarks loved by residents and visitors alike, and the trades and crafts still being practiced.

This new volume, *Thornham – Then and Now* combines the aspects of the previous two books through a collection of new photographs and previously unpublished old photographs and postcards which have come to light since *Thornham, a Photographic Portrait* was published. For this volume, I was joined by Stephen Greef, whose family has lived in the village for generations. Stephen's father, Henry, is well remembered as the Post Master and the Thornham correspondent for the *Lynn News*; his uncle Desmond played the organ in the church for many years. Stephen discovered a total of more than eighty scrapbooks which Henry had kept over many years. These recorded just about any event which took place in the village going back to the opening of the Drill Hall in 1907. Sadly, many of the scrapbooks were water damaged, but we have rescued what we can. Mandy Sadler did a similar project when she was at the village school and has kindly allowed us to use her collections.

The theme of this book is continuity and change. Many Thornham residents, whether they have lived here for ten or a hundred years, profess to love the village for the peace, tranquility and slow pace of life which it offers - while the reality is that they are surrounded by change. Building, particularly infilling, continues apace, as do issues with planners when new designs often seem unsympathetic to the existing style. The old village

◀ An Edwardian picnic on Thornham beach. In the background, the few men present appear to be sparring.

shop has given way to a thriving Thornham Deli complex which continues to develop; the old mushroom farm at Drove Farm is now a fast developing range of retail outlets; the Lifeboat and The Chequers are part of Marco Pierre White's "Wheelers of St. James' chain". The much loved, but by now inadequate, Drill Hall has been sold and the village now has a six- acre playing field complete with soccer, cricket and tennis facilities. The new village hall opened in 2013 and is serving the village just as well as the old Drill Hall did for a hundred years. The offshore wind farm can be seen clearly when the atmospheric conditions are right.

The influx of second home owners, visitors and caravanners continues, and they all contribute to the community life of the village. The days of reliance on agriculture have long gone – Henry Bett employed fifty-five workers on Thornham Farms; his son Stephen employs two! They have been largely replaced by the tourist industry, but the current mix works well. There are many activities, new and old, from Bowls, which has now reached its centenary, to the Village Cinema, and live satellite theatre, which ensure that Thornham remains a desirable village in which to live.

Doubtless, the pace of change will continue and this book will need a substantial revision before many more years have passed.

John Warham
Thornham 2015

▶ The Granaries, Coal Barn and the *Jessie Mary*.

THORNHAM.

A Coastal Village
The Harbour

In 1845 Thornham was described in White's Directory as 'a large village, pleasantly seated near the salt marshes, with a population of some 790'. The sea originally came up as far as the village where there was a natural harbour – the sea is now a mile or more away over the marshes. The Dutchman, van Haesdoncke, supervised the draining of some of the marsh and increased the capacity of the harbour, hence 'Dutchman's Hill' just off The Green.

Before the arrival of the railway line at Hunstanton in 1887, the village's main connection with places beyond was through the harbour. Trading vessels took outgoing goods, mainly grain, to Newcastle and Hull, with coal and other essential supplies arriving at the Coal Barn.

Nathaniel Woods built the sluice in the harbour to try to combat silting in the channel, but to no avail and the village turned its attention to the land, and later, the tourist and holiday trade.

▶ *Jessie Mary* berthed in Thornham harbour by the Coal Barn with the Granary in the background.

Thornham Harbour

▲ Builder Robert Howell, aboard his boat *Sally*, with Mark Rix.

◄ Thornham Oysters was a successful business which closed down in 2010 when Ken and Kath Haywood moved to Titchwell.

▲ All sorts of pleasure craft still use the harbour. Antony Needham and Vic Hardy take *Glimmer* on a rare sailing outing.

THORNHAM OYSTERS
01485 512163

TILLY
LOWESTOFT

The Sluice

The sluice was built in an attempt to keep the channel from silting up. The sluice gate was closed at high tide and reopened at low tide so that the outgoing rush of water would help clear the channel. It took three men some twenty minutes to operate the sluice gate, but it was all a losing battle which the silt eventually won.

THORNHAM.

ALL SAINTS'.—On Sunday after the service an organ recital was given by friends in the district.

OLD CUSTOM REVIVED.—About fifty years ago, near the old granaries, a very large sluice was used for holding up the water at high tides. At low water the sluice was hauled up and the harbour was cleared of the mud. By this means large cargo vessels could be landed near the hard road. A few days ago a number of men employed by Mrs. Ames-Lyde with chains and pulleys set this old sluice in working order, and so it is hoped the harbour will be deepened.

FEMALE SUFFRAGE.—In spite of the fact that the village is emphatically opposed to the women's suffrage movement, a Miss Brackenbury held a meeting in support thereof the other evening near the Jubilee Tree. After the usual abuse of the Government, questions were invited. An affirmative reply was given to the enquiry, "Do you think breaking windows and doing wilful damage assist your cause?" "The public know we are in earnest," said the speaker.

▲ The sluice in 1913 after maintenance work had been carried out. The newspaper cutting of the period describes its operation.

The Marshes

At the beginning of 2015, shooting rights on the marsh are held by the Kent Wildfowling and Conservation Association, replacing the Thornham Wildfowlers Association who shot here for many years.

The marshes are also a popular haunt of waders and geese, particularly during the winter months.

THORNHAM & DISTRICT WILDFOWLERS ASSOCIATION

MEMBERSHIP CARD

Hon. Secretary:
G. C. Bussey,
Honora,
The Green,
Thornham,
Hunstanton,
Norfolk.

Hon Treasurer:
A. Sadler,
Church St.,
Thornham,
Hunstanton,
Norfolk.

▲ The wreck of the Northern Prince by the harbour in the 1980s.
It was eventually taken apart and moved away.

▲ The tidal surge of December 2013 removed this much
photographed wreck and deposited it a further mile into the
centre of the marsh.

The Coal Barn

Situated on a small patch of raised land, the Coal Barn has been used as a store, a film set and perhaps, in the near future, will be a holiday home.

The Coal Barn was sold in 2006 with planning permission for use as an art studio for six months of the year. This never came about and the building is on the market again. Now the intention is to convert it into a holiday home although, to date, the planners have refused permission.

◀ In the nineteenth century there would have been brewers in the village, but porter and stout, the popular drinks of the day, were brewed in London, brought to Thornham by sea and, it is said, stored in the Coal Barn.

The Coal Barn, Thornham Harbour

▼ The Coal Barn 'disguised' as Pip's house for BBC Television's adaptation of Charles Dickens' *Great Expectations* in 1998.

BBC's Dickens of a film at Thornham and Holme

FILMING for a new BBC period drama based on Charles Dickens' Great Expectations novel starts in Thornham and Holme on Sunday.

Over the past week, the BBC's technical team has been making temporary cosmetic changes to the landscape along Thornham Harbour to create a mid-1800s setting, including the revamp of the coal barn so it looks like a smithy.

Actor Bernard Hill – who starred as Scouse hardman Yosser "Gissa Job" Hughes in the 1980's drama Boys from the Blackstuff, and more recently as the Captain in the Oscar-winning Titanic – will be among the actors on location when filming takes place from Sunday to Wednesday.

The five scenes being filmed will feature the outside of the coal barn, the sea wall path, the harbour landing stages, and the marshes and mud flats of Holme Dunes Nature Reserve.

The Thornham scenes will feature Pip as a boy.

The drama stars Charlotte Rampling as Miss Havisham, Bernard Hill as the convict Magwich, and Ioan Gruffuud, star of the new Hornblower series, plays Pip as a man. It is scheduled to be broadcast as two-part dramatisation in the spring on BBC2.

The Granary

The Granary and Coal Barn were both built by George Hogge (the son of William Hogge who built the Red House, the School and the Hall). There were two granaries originally. One was demolished early in the twentieth century and the other after the great floods of 1953. At one stage it was owned by Nathaniel Woods whose boat the *Jessie Mary* was the last to trade in Thornham's harbour.

◀ There are many theories as to what these stumps actually were. Perhaps they acted as stays in the harbour at the back of the Granary?

▲ The upper floor of the Granary was once used as an artist's studio. Before the Second World War, families spent their summer holidays there.

The Mill

The Crane family were flour millers in Thornham for at least three generations in the eighteenth and early nineteenth centuries. The mill stopped operating after the death of Elizabeth Crane in 1900.

With the summer harvest safely gathered in, the women and girls of nineteenth-century Thornham gleaned the fields, gathering up any ears of corn left behind. They would thresh the ears themselves and then take the corn to the village miller to be ground into baking flour.

One of a series of pew ends in Thornham All Saints' Church depicting various trades as well as the sins of drunkenness, anger and laziness.

3210. THE MILL & HARBOUR. THORNHAM.

Model-maker Mr Kenneth Hamlin with his scale replica of Thornham windmill — now on display in the local church. (UC 6571).

Windmill model for church

A WINDMILL that once graced the skyline of Thornham has been recreated in scale model form by a retired banker and now stands in the local church.

The model, built almost entirely of wood, was lovingly fashioned over two years by Mr Kenneth Hamlin, of Station Road, Heacham.

Mr Hamlin became interested in windmills when he joined a group of DIY enthusiasts in a mill restoration project in the Sussex village of Nutley.

"When I moved up to West Norfolk five years ago I discovered that there had been a composite mill at Thornham — one of only three or four built in this country," he said.

The mill was originally situated on Beacon Hill, but was moved down to the harbour area to be more convenient for farmers transporting their produce.

"I think it probably fell into disuse at the turn of the century. All that remains of it today is the brick base and two small sections at Gressenhall Museum.

"Because I was going to build a scale model it was necessary so take measurements of the brick base and the figure at the museum before drawing up any plans.

"Only one elderly village resident remembered the mill when it was working, but luckily I was sent some old photographs that helped me with my work.

"It took almost two years to complete the model — much of that time being taken up with paperwork in calculating the dimensions of various parts.

"When it was finished I didn't really want to keep it at home, so I offered it to the church at Thornham. They decided that it needed to be protected in a glass case and that is why it hasn't been on display earlier."

▲ A model of the mill, made by Kenneth Hamlin of Heacham, is displayed in the parish church.

▼ The circular base is all that now remains. A notice attached to it used to warn: *Admission to this field is free. The Bull will charge later.*

▲ The mill workings were dismantled around 1930. It is said that some of the working parts were taken to a museum in Norwich.

Stacks at Manor Farm.

◄ Aerial view of Manor Farm taken in 1965 before it was converted into residential and holiday homes. Billy Walker's petrol station can be seen in the foreground.

▼ The former farm buildings are now let for holidays.

A Farming Village

There were several farms in the village. The Hall and Manor Farms were tenanted by the Heading family. The Betts farmed Malt House, Jones' and Ling Farms and Vic Helsdon had Dairy Farm. With the decline of agriculture, movement away from the village began. Some emigrated to Canada, while a group of Thornham families moved to the north east, looking for work in the coal and steel industries. Descendants of former Thornham villages, including the May family, still live in Cleveland.

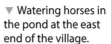

◀ Thomas Jones with one of his horses.

▼ Watering horses in the pond at the east end of the village.

▲ Joe Taylor, owner of Thornham Ling farm in the 1930s, with Bob Riseborough, farm manager.

▲ Haytime by floodlight.

▲ They look like telegraph poles that are being shifted, but the cart seems too small.

▶ There used to be two blacksmiths/farriers; one was run by Jimmy Tipple in Forge Lane just off the High Street, the other by Samson Yaxley down the path leading to the Bowling Club. This has been extended and converted into a second home.

▶ Eric Beck and Neville Nudds worked together for more than forty years on Thornham Farms.

◀ Luan Walker driving, pulling a reaper-binder, the machine which preceded the combine harvester.

▶ Joe Bush, foreman for Henry Bett at Thornham Farms from 1947 to the 1960s.

◀ Jack Middleton and other workers at Ian Hopper's mushroom farm, which is now the site of Drove Farm Orchards.

▲ Stacking boxes of mushrooms.

◀ Sowing the mushrooms, Ian Hopper on the right.

▲ The transport of farm produce along the main road is still a regular sight. These are potato boxes.

◀ Drove Farm Orchards.

The Shoot

Shooting parties are a regular part of the winter scene at Thornham Hall. Pheasant and red-legged partridge are the main game.

▲ A 1920s shooting party.

▶ A game dealer's receipt for rabbits and hares, 1972.

▲ An army surplus truck carries the beaters out to the drives.

▶ Victor Ames (centre) with a shooting party, c. 1900.

▲ Hugh Andrew about to set his ferret on the trail of a rabbit in the 1970s.

▶ Bob Riches with Gunner.

▼ Chris Hill has been the gamekeeper since 2007.

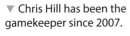

▶ Chris Cotton, Peter Jackson and Jimmy Groom.

Thornham Trades
The Ironworks

Edith Ames Lyde's initial idea for the ironworks had been to create an evening pastime for villagers. But the business took off and Edith formed the company, Ames-Lyde, Elsum & Co to market the ironwork at home and around the world. The works closed in 1916.

◄ Mrs Ames Lyde's brother-in-law, Victor Ames, worked up the designs at Thornham ironworks.

▲ Noah Francis (extreme left, front row) was a talented iron worker.

Thornham . . . .
Wrought Ironwork

ILLUSTRATED
CATALOGUE. .

Photographs of
Work executed

V. A

AMES-LYDE, ELSUM & Co.,

THORNHAM, KING'S LYNN,
NORFOLK.

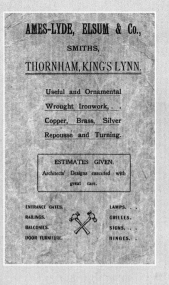

AMES-LYDE, ELSUM & Co.,

SMITHS,

THORNHAM, KING'S LYNN.

Useful and Ornamental
Wrought Ironwork, . .
Copper, Brass, Silver
Repousse and Turning.

ESTIMATES GIVEN.
Architects' Designs executed with
great care.

ENTRANCE GATES.   LAMPS. . .
RAILINGS.   GRILLES.
BALCONIES.   SIGNS. . .
DOOR FURNITURE.   HINGES. .

'In these days, when the wall of unemployment rises throughout the land, and the competition of the foreigner is so stern that some people desire to restrict it by prohibitive tariffs, surely this little tale of heroic achievement and the wresting of an industry from the hands of the Continental artisan, is something to record.'

From the *Sunday at Home*, a family magazine for sabbath reading published by the Religious Trust Society, about 1910.

Pages from the Ironworks catalogue.

▲ The King's Head sign was made at Thornham Ironworks.

◄ The iron rose made by Noah Francis to give to his wife.

▲ The decorative hinges shown here were made for a design by Sir Edwin Lutyens. They are now in The Pleasaunce, Overstrand.

The Kings Head

◀ Iron workers in 1905. The photograph includes co-founder and schoolmaster William Elsum, Walter Potter and Reggie Allen, the boy (centre) with the watch chain. Reggie became office clerk at the works.

▲ Vic Hardy keeps the Thornham Ironworks tradition going in his workshop off the High Street. Vic made all the weathervanes on this page including the two above which are at Coastguard Cottages.

▶ The caravan weathervane (opposite) was made by fifteen year old John Whiting for his parents, Tony and Ann, keen caravanners.

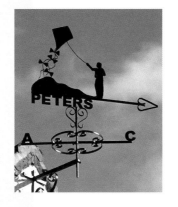

The Garage

There was still a village garage until late in the twentieth century. It eventually closed and has been converted into a holiday home.

▲ At work in the 1920s.

▲ The staff in the '50s. (left to right) Len Farr, Bill Jacobs, Ray Francis, Mary Jacobs, Jim Jacobs, Mrs Jacobs Senior, Jimmy Rix and Ronnie Scales. Other owners included Vic and Sue Hardy, Ken and Kath Hayward, Dave Smalls, Bill Tollerton, Mr King and Mr Parker, and Noel Gosling, who had the garage in the '30s and '40s.

▲ The garage was run by Vic and Sue Hardy in the 1980s.

▲ The garage in 1961.

THORNHAM

A four bedroom house with attached village general store and large workshop to the rear.
£145,000

Builders

Reg Needham and his wife, Ivy, moved to Norfolk from London after the war, eventually settling in Thornham where Reg set up his building firm. His sons John, a carpenter and Antony, a builder, still work in the village carrying on their father's legacy.

R. H. NEEDHAM

Builders and Contractors

★

ELECTRICAL   GENERAL BUILDERS
PLUMBERS

★

Thornham – King's Lynn

Telephone : THORNHAM 230

▲ Reg Needham.

The lych gate was built by Tim Siddle and Henry Cobb in memory of Nathaniel Woods and was opened by Woods' daughter, Maggie Page.

◀ Maggie Page opening the new gate in 1971.

TO THE MEMORY OF
NATHANIEL WOODS, 1862–1936
THE LAST MERCHANT TO USE THE PORT OF THORNHAM
MARY ANN AGNES HIS WIFE 1863–1937
CHARLES WILLIAM THEIR SON 1897–1918
KILLED IN ACTION IN FRANCE

Village Shops
The Market Place

It's now just a tricky and busy bend in the main road, but these pictures show that it was indeed the centre and market place of the village in times gone by. Church, pub, village green and Ducker's Stores are all within a hundred yards of each other.

Market Place, Thornham.

▲ One of the Ducker's shops in the village, this sold earthenware and ironmongery, as well as sweets and chocolate. Formerly London House, it is now renamed Calendar House and is a holiday home.

Ducker's Stores and Church Street, Thornham

◄ The Ducker sales team and dog. The plate on the door advertises an agency for Norwich Union insurance.

▲ James William Ducker, his wife Jane and their sons James and Cyril.

The Duckers must have been the retail entrepreneurs of their day, having three stores in the village.

High Street, Thornham. (*Ducker's Series.*) J 2905.

Stocks Hill House

Stocks Hill House was the grocery store of Johnson & Back before becoming Henry and Amy Wyett's butcher's shop. It was later an antique shop run by Mark Wyett and is now Phil and Nicola Peters' family home. Bob le Masurier, whose collection of postcards appears widely in this book, lived here with his wife, Barbara.

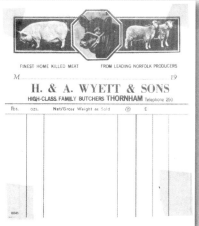

▲ Daphne Siddle stops for a chat outside the shop with Amy Wyett.

◀ Johnson and Back's Grocery Stores. Note the cow crossing the road in front of the King's Head on its way from Dairy Farm to graze on the marsh.

▲ Roger Drewry, Eddie Ayton and Mark Wyett.

The Post Office

Alfred and Anna Greef (née Moorhouse) moved to Thornham in the early 1900s, Alfred to work as a gardener at the Manor House, Anna to look after the Rev Moore's daughter, Winifred. They took over the Drapery Stores in Priory House in 1927. The Post Office was acquired in 1936 after the death of the previous Postmistress Mrs Ducker. Henry Greef took over the running of the Post Office in 1971. Henry continued to run the Post Office at Priory House until about 1977 when it moved to Victoria House opposite the school.

▲ Johnsons the drapers in the early 1920s.

THE OBSERVER 4
LONDON, E.C.4
RECEIVING AGENT
KING'S LYNN
Car to THORNHAM
03.10 L'pool St.   CONTRACT
BAKER

Unit   NEWS OF THE WORLD Receiving Agent
KING'S LYNN
SPECIAL TRUCK.
Liverpool St. 3.10 a.m.
Then by CAR to   Van No.
Mrs. Baker,   4
THORNHAM

▲ The Sunday newspapers would arrive at King's Lynn station by train from London before being transported to Thornham.

▲ Anna and Alfred Greef outside their Drapery Stores. Anna is holding their son Henry.

MR HENRY GREEF, village postmaster at Thornham moving back to Victoria House (RC 3558).

◄ Henry Greef, all wrapped up and ready to do his round, 1963.

► The Post Office was based in Victoria House from the mid 1970s.

The Bakery

The Bakery on Church Street served as a general store, bakery and Post Office fulfilling many of the needs of villagers and holiday makers alike. Run by Martin and Judith Proffitt in the 1990s, it closed in 2004 and is now an annexe of the Orange Tree pub.

L. & O. FISHER

BAKERS — GROCERS

CONFECTIONERS — TOBACCONIST

★

The Bakery, Church Street

Thornham – King's Lynn – Norfolk

Telephone : Thornham 264

The New Village Shop/Deli

Thornham Deli was built in 2006 by local builder 'Spider' Goddard. A large extension was completed in 2014 and more retail outlets added.

KLN•A.
24.2.06

Thornham shop nears completion

THORNHAM'S village shop and post office is taking shape and in line for completion by the end of March.

Since work started around September last year, the building's shell is now complete, and all that needs to be done includes laying floor tiling, fitting a staircase, and adding doors and skirting boards.

"It's finishing-off jobs," said Michael "Spider" Goddard, who owns the land on which the facility has been built, and is paying for it to be constructed with his wife, Margaret.

The car park also needs to be completed, and an entrance needs to be surfaced.

Mr Goddard has done some of the work himself, including adding soak-

aways and putting in patio areas.

He said: "We tried to make it look like a traditional old barn. We've used old roof tiles, and I'm really pleased how it's turned out."

The walls of the shop, which will include manager's accommodation upstairs, are made of brick and chalk.

Mr Goddard did not want to say how much the project cost, but said: "It's been quite an expensive build, but everything's been what I've expected it to be."

Once complete the shop will be rented by Mr Goddard to business partners Mrs Patti Gambling and Miss Tania Rowell, who will also run the post office.

And Mr Goddard is looking forward to seeing it up and running.

He said: "It's vital. There are a lot of old people in the village, and it's a good social hub for those who don't see people.

"It's good for holiday people too. It really does make village life."

Thornham's post office and shop were housed in The Old Bakery, Church Street, until it closed in 2003.

A group of residents got together to try to buy it, but the premises were taken off the market.

A committee then looked at 17 sites where a new facility could be built, but found none were suitable, and took up Mr Goddard's offer of building the facility on his land.

▲ The Deli site was developed in 2014 when Jeanne Whittome (top right) and Janie Thompson (centre right) took over the business. The new-look Deli has been extended and refurbished to create a new style shop which includes a patisserie, bakery and delicatessen. Manager, Denise LeGallez (bottom left) and Executive Chef Gemma Arnold (bottom right) complete the team.

▲ Barefoot Retreats, run by Annelli Taylor, Helen Millin (left) and Emma Tagg (right), opened its stylish office on the extended Deli site in October 2014. It specialises in marketing luxury holiday cottages along the north Norfolk coast.

The Butcher's Shop

Once a butcher's shop, York House was also used as the showroom for Thornham ironworks.

The Hair Factory

Lynette Bailey has run The Hair Factory since 1982 when she started her first business. The salon has expanded since its early days and now offers a wide range of hair and beauty treatments for all. Lynette's niece, Jo Toop, has worked here for more than ten years.

◀ Tommy and Ada Haines (left) ran the butcher's shop in York House. There was an abatoir at the back.

◀ Jo Toop, Lynette Bailey and Lucy Cole.

The mobile fish & chips van was a popular feature in the village for many years, with queues forming every Wednesday at 5 pm. It hasn't been seen in the village since 2012.

Bryan and Carol Read (top) and Michael and Jenny Partyka (below).

The Pubs

At a time when pubs up and down the country are closing their doors at an alarming rate, Thornham is lucky to have three thriving establishments, underpinned by the increasing amount of tourist trade. The pubs of today may be a far cry from the ale houses of a bygone age, but they all provide excellent dining facilities. The Lifeboat and The Chequers are both part of Marco Pierre White's 'Wheelers of St. James' chain, while Mark Goode's Orange Tree, the former King's Head, is a regular winner of awards for pub dining in Norfolk, under head chef Phil Milner.

The Lifeboat

The Lifeboat Inn was originally a working farm and beer house. Renamed The Lifeboat in the nineteenth century, it was run by the Sadler family from 1869 until the 1930s. Setch Brewery in King's Lynn belonged to the Hogge family and was taken over by Bullards of Norwich in 1928.

▼ Nellie Sadler outside The Lifeboat in about 1860.

56

▲ Before the conservatory was built at the back.

THE LIFEBOAT, THORNHAM

▲ These photographs show the inside of The Lifeboat when Ossie Waterfield was the landlord. He restyled the pub in the mid 1950s with furniture and artifacts bought from antique sales. It might have been the first overhaul The Lifeboat underwent.

▲ Fraser, Joan and Vernon Maldoom outside The Lifeboat in 1962. The Maldooms are descendants of the Sadler family, former Lifeboat owners.

◄ Olive & Ossie Waterfield became landlords in 1950.

▲ Lynne and Nick Handley were landlords of The Lifeboat in the 1980s.

▲ 'Pennies in the Hole' is now seldom played – the objective is to throw thirteen pennies into the hole without a miss, for the prize of a bottle of whisky. Long serving landlord Ossie Waterfield claimed he only saw it done once in his time.

▼ The bench with 'Pennies in the Hole'.

▲ Head Chef 'Stork' Chamberlain with General Manager Helen Stafford.

6284. THE CAMPING GROUND, THORNHAM

◀ The field behind The Lifeboat in the 1950s when it was owned by Sonny Middleton.

THE HAVEN
CARAVAN PARK
McDonnell
☎ 01553 636243/636279

McDonnell
Caravans
THE HAVEN
CARAVAN PARK
01553 636243

◀ Mike McDonnell.

ENQUIRIES   SALES

▲ Tom and Sylvia Webb have been wardens at The Haven Caravan Park since 2004. They can be found, during the season, at No. 66.

Caravans

Mike McDonnell's caravan park business started in 1983, with The Haven, formerly known as the Milkman's Site, purchased from Mrs Middleton. In 1986, the park at the back of The Lifeboat was acquired, and the site at the back of The Chequers was added in 1992. There are just under 150 caravan holiday homes, which are all 'state of the art' and provide their owners with many enjoyable holidays and happy memories over the years.

The Orange Tree

The former King's Head is probably the oldest pub in the village and is situated, as are many village pubs, in close proximity to the church. It was renamed The Orange Tree in 2005. It is run by Mark and Jo Goode and their team, including prize winning chef Phil Milner, and is a popular restaurant. The OT also has rooms in the Old Bakery and former village shop, next door.

King's Head Hotel
THORNHAM . NORFOLK

Menu

Mine Hosts: JOHN & PAT HOUGHTON

▲ Roger Fitzpatrick, landlord from 1958 to 1962, with Doris Smith (née Bell) and chef Jozef Partyka.

▲ John George Parrinder Wilson, landlord from 1937 to 1957.

▲ Head Chef, Phil Milner.

▶ The pub always had a reputation for good food in the village, going back to its days as The King's Head. Here is a typical menu from the 1970s. Note the prices!

BIN	WINES	full	half
	RED BURGUNDY		
1	Beaujolais	1.20	65p
2	Beaune	1.70	90p
3	Nuits St. George	1.70	90p
	RED BORDEAUX		
6	St. Emilion	1.25	65p
	WHITE BORDEAUX		
8	Graves	1.20	65p
9	Sauternes	1.40	75p
	WHITE BURGUNDY		
12	Chablis	1.45	75p
	MOSELLE		
15	Berncasteler	1.20	65p
	YUGOSLAVIAN		
16	Yugoslav Riesling	1.05	55p
	PORTUGUESE		
17	Mateus Rosé	1.40	75p
	CHAMPAGNE		
19	Lanson Black Label	3.00	1.50p
	RED or WHITE WINE	19p per glass	

▶ Current landlord Mark Goode and his wife Jo. Chris Neal and Daniel Gibson are the Bar Managers who keep the beer flowing.

The Old School Room (or Reading Room) beside the King's Head was used as a classroom in the old days and became a regular venue for Parish Council meetings. It was the Home Guard HQ in the early years of the Second World War.

When it had its side knocked out by two large road working machines it had to be demolished.

◄ Advertisement from 1986.

▲ Jake and Ann John were the last landlords of The King's Head before its name was changed.

The Chequers

The Chequers Inn was a popular local for many years. It was known as The Old Coach house between 2004 and 2013 when it reverted to The Chequers.

4371.   Chequers Inn, Thornham.

▲ Edward E Bell landlord c. 1930

▲ Richard Sidey and his dog Champagne. Richard was landlord of The Chequers in the 1970s.

▲ Bill and Nancy Scrouther were landlords in the early 1950s.

▼ Butcher Harry Wyett, Billy Howard, Tony Petchey, Reg Needham, Bobbie Bocking, Ben Howard and Randall Pearce.

▲ J H Page landlord c. 1912

▲ Chris Dyson and friends joining in Christmas carols at The Chequers.

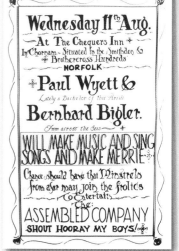

▲ Villagers, including Mark Wyett, 'Spider' Goddard (top), Arthur 'Ricky' Richmond (centre right), and Reg Needham (above) celebrate the visit of HMS Thornham crew.

▲ Murals painted by a customer in the 1960s.

▲ Local popular musician and songwriter Paul Wyett has lived and worked in Munich for many years.

▲ The Chequers was traditionally the starting point for the annual Sponsored Walk to raise funds for the village hall and playing field.

▲ After nearly ten years as The Coach House, the pub reverted to its former name, The Chequers, in 2013 under the ownership of Marco Pierre White.

▶ David Jackson is the senior musician and Bagman of the King's Morris.

The King's Morris have been popular visitors to Thornham for many years. These photos show the annual 'Walking Tour of Thornham' when Morris dancers from the whole of East Anglia visit the village, to dance and later to sing in The Lifeboat. Jill Bennett plays the violin.

MORRIS DANCING on Easter Monday

THE KING'S MORRIS of King's Lynn

Monday 13 April 2009
Snettisham, The Rose & Crown 11.30am
Heacham, Norfolk Lavender 12.30pm
Thornham, The Lifeboat Inn 1.30pm

Bagman: David Jackson, 9 Edward Street, King's Lynn PE30 5QS
Telephone 01553 768930   E-mail paljac7@yahoo.co.uk

▶ Ian Heighton, official Fool, with Norman the Konkerer.

Fun and Games
Cricket

Village cricket is still very much a part of the summer scene. The new pitch is now firmly established on the playing field as one of the best facilities in the area. In a link with the past, the old wooden pavilion was manually moved from the old field on The Green.

▲ In the early days cricket in the village was played on this pitch in The Park adjoining Thornham Hall.

Feby . 8 1905

THORNHAM. — CRICKET CLUB. — The members had their annual meeting at Howard's room on Wednesday evening, preceded by a tea, the chair being taken by the captain (Mr. G. Heading), who subsequently gave place to the vicar (Rev. W. H. Waller). The loyal toasts having been honoured, the Chairman proposed "The Secretary," eulogising the work he had done, and referring to the great help given by the captain. The secretary, after returning thanks, submitted his report for the past year. This shewed that the club played 26 matches during last season, and won the majority of them. In the Sandringham District League competition they won 6 out of 9 matches. The club numbered 40 members, and they had been able sometimes to play first and second eleven matches on the same day. They finished the year with a balance of 3/3½ on the right side. The best batting and bowling averages were by Mr. Southerland, Haynes and Yaxley being second and third in the batting averages. He proposed "Success to the Thornham Cricket Club," coupled with the name of Mr. G. Heading, who replied, and proposed the health of the treasurer (Mr. W. H. Elsum), who was absent. Mr. Helsdon proposed "The Vicar," who returned thanks ; and Mr. Southerland proposed "The Visitors," for whom Mr. Scott responded. Songs were sung by the Vicar, Messrs. Webster, Asker jun., Hines, Collison, Tipple, Yaxley, Scott, Bridges and Milton ; and short recitations were contributed by the Vicar and Mr. Asker sen.

▲ A championship Thornham cricket side. (left to right) back row: Charlie Williamson, unidentified, Charlie Hunt, unidentified, Reg Carter, Donny Woods, Reggie Rayner; front row: Philip Anderson, Benny Howard, Eddie Bell, Laddie Frohawk and Harry Bustin.

▲ The hairstyles identify this clearly as a Thornham CC team of the 1970s.

Thornham bowler Ross Bray hurls down a delivery under the watchful gaze of Hunstanton II batsman M. Cornell.

Picture: ALAN MILLER (97/07/31)

Scoreboard

Hunstanton II		Division Six
		Thornham
S. Jones c b Williamson	11	R. Bray b Charnley 0
M. Cornell c b Williamson	11	R. Williamson c b Kurley 2
J. Pekszyc run out	12	B. Hare c b Charnley 2
J. Eaton c b Childs	14	M. Childs b Kurley 6
T. Milsom c b Childs	8	A. Burt b Kurley 10
A. Searle b Harper	11	R. Hinds b Charnley 1
D. Sayers not out	43	J. Harper b Charnley 6
M. Charnley b Burt	46	M. Williamson not out 13
P. Dennis not out	7	N. Chapman b Charnley 6
Extras	24	K. Pooley c & b Charnley 11
Total (7 wkts)	187	K. Hinds b Clarke 0
		Extras 7
		Total (all out) 64

Bowling: R. Williamson 12-2-26-2; R. Bray 12-1-34-0; M. Childs 9-0-57-2; S. Harper 7-1-43-1; A. Burt 3-0-16-1; B. Hare 2-0-10-0.

Bowling: M. Charnley 9-2-33-6; D. Kurley 5-1-18-3; G. Clarke 3.4-0-9-1.

The annual challenge match between the Club and the Veterans is always a popular event.

▲ Long serving opening batsman Adrian 'Sid' Siddle. Adrian spends most of his spare time keeping the wicket in top class condition.

▲ Thornham CC at the start of the first season on the new playing field in 2011.

▲ Moving the pavilion to the new playing field.

▲ Club Secretary, former captain and mainstay of Thornham cricket, Ron Williamson, lovingly coaxing the old roller into life.

TOP BOWLER

Ron Williamson (Thornham CC)

The wily Ron Williamson proved the matchwinner in Thornham's victory over Dereham B at the weekend. Williamson picked up 7 for 26 with the ball as Dereham, chasing 252 for victory, fell 113 runs short of their victory target.

Soccer

Thornham FC flourished in the 1950s and '60s. Sadly the Club had to be disbanded in the 1970s because of lack of support. 2013 saw soccer back in Thornham with an enthusiastic team playing again in the Norfolk League Division 3.

▼ A pre-Second World War Thornham football side. (left to right), back row George Wilson, landlord of the King's Head, Marshall 'Nitch' Riseborough (father of Shirley Lake), Luan Walker, Charlie Riseborough, Dave Stimpson, Tom Lake, Charlie Hunt and Philip Anderson; front row: unidentified, Billy Walker, Eddie Riseborough, Reg Carter, Charlie Goff, uncle of June (née Goff) Fryett, and Darny Mahoney.

Footall — Thornham Minors Football Club held a crazy football match when parents and friends played against the club. A total sum of £34.75 was raised for club funds.

▲ Marshall Riseborough also played football for the Linnets in King's Lynn.

▲ 1950s. Back row: Eddie Riseborough, Paul Skillings, Dick Johnson, George Misson, ? McFadyen, Harry Johnson (from Brancaster), Reg Baker; front row: Freddie Frohawk, Ivan Bell, George Raven, Peter Smith, Reg Carter and Gordon Johnson.

▲ Back row: Henry Bett, Timothy Arnold, Clive Johnson, Simon Rix, Mark Floyd, Cecil Rix, Howard Floyd, Mark Rix, Adrian Siddle and an official; front row: Jonathon Kipling, Sam Cook, Paul Rumbellow and Jeremy and Stephen Lake.

▲ 1960s. Back row: Gordon Lake, Malcolm Emmerson, Bruce Jongman, Jimmy Janz and Cecil Rix; front row: John Hipkin, John Potter, Alan Walden, Colin Walker, Leo Dolman and Don Playford.

▲ Back row: Brian Hipkin, Simon Housden, Tim Burgess, Mark Rix, Cecil Rix, Robert Hinds, Steve Walker; front row: Simon Rix, Andrew Burt, Adam Bird, Stephen Lake, Ron Williamson, Charlie Needham and John Whiting.

▲ Back in action after a gap of more than thirty years. The line-up for Thornham's first game in 2013 after re-forming.

Saturday 21st September 2013

Kick-Off 2:30 pm

Thornham F.C

v

Greyfriars

North West Norfolk League Division 3

Thornham Playing Field

Bowls

The Bowls Club plays on a picturesque, secluded site in the centre of the village just off the High Street. The club celebrated its centenary in 2014.

Eighteen members of Thornham Bowls Club attended the annual meeting at The Chequers Inn, Thornham. Officers elected were: A. E. Richmond, chairman; T. Lewin, vice-chairman; and the remaining officers were re-elected en-bloc with the addition of Mr J. King to serve on the selection committee, general committee and Drill Hall committee.

The treasurer Mr F. Bayden showed a balance of £497 in his report. Samantha and Joanne Coates volunteered to raise funds for Thornham Church and the bowls club with a sponsored horse ride.

The meeting agreed to join the Docking League and it was also agreed that only one open day should be held during the coming season.

▲ A Thornham bowls team. Back row (left to right)): Tom Lake, Billy Johnson, Harry Walker, the Rev Rushmer, Billy Porter, Lewis Mitchell, Arthur Back; middle row: Billy Tipple, Percy Proudfoot, George Raven, George Lee, Vic Helsdon, Benny Howard; front row: Harry Bell, Bob Thompson, Jack Walker, Stephen Hewitt.

▲ Peter Goff doing the measuring.

▲ Open Day at the
Bowls Club, July 1996.

◀ Stalwart member of
Thornham Bowls Club,
Tony Whiting keeping the
green in top condition.

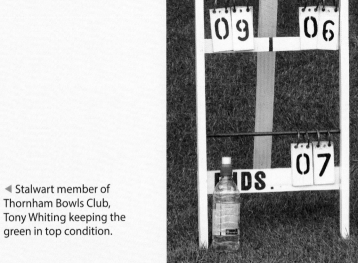

Music on the Field

The new playing field is the centre of much social and community activity during the summer months. The annual Music on the Field Festival, started by Monica Clare and Phil Warne, is an established part of the Thornham Summer Calendar.

Colin Venes relaxes with a pint while others enjoy the sunshine and the music.

Prize shooting and Clays

The Vicar in 1912 encouraged the men of the village as follows, 'There are two types of men in this country, those who can shoot, the others are women'.

▼ Children entertain the women with country dancing at the 1910 Prize Shooting. The men are mostly seated at picnic tables in the background.

▲ Victor Ames

"MORRIS DANCING",
THORNHAM PRIZE SHOOTING, 1910

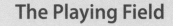

Playing field opened

Gala day washed out

The day that Thornham playing field fund committee had been planning and working for the past six months was virtually washed out by rain on Sunday when the grand carnival-style gala, organised to mark the official opening of the playing field, was washed out by rain.

The five-a-side football tournament involving eight teams from local villages was postponed, and nearly all the other activities cancelled. Radio Norfolk personality Keith Skipper still performed the opening ceremony but it was held instead in the drill hall, where several stalls had been set up.

Mr. Chris Smith, a member of the committee, said: "We had hoped to raise between £500 and £600, to buy a children's adventure climbing frame for the playing field but we probably won't get anywhere near half that now. It is very disappointing after all the hard work."

In the evening a "folk nite" was held in the drill hall, featuring Paul Wyett, a professional folk singer, now resident in Munich, Germany, whose brother Mark is chairman of the playing field fund committee.

It is hoped to stage the football tournament for which medals have already been bought, on August bank holiday Sunday.

● **Some of the committee of the Thornham Playing Field Association and helpers on their new field which was officially opened on Sunday.**

▲ A clay pigeon shoot at one of Thornham Manor garden fêtes when Mr Robarts was in residence. (left to right) Dick Batterbee, Vic Helsdon, Arthur (Ricky) Richmond, David Sutherland and Vincent Sadler.

Clay pigeon shoot helps eye camps

A day of clay pigeon shooting at Thornham raised around £150 for Rotary Club eye camps in India.

Mr. Chris Swain, secretary of Hunstanton Rotary, which organised yesterday's event, said the club and the 60 participants were so satisfied they wanted to make it an annual event.

Raising money for materials and staff for the eye camps was ongoing, Mr. Swain explained. £90 was enough to set up one such camp in India, where some Rotary members were surgeons.

The event attracted competitors from West Norfolk and the Midlands. Mr. K. A. Ellis, of Whittlesey, emerged as the best shot of the day and received the high gun award. Runner-up was Mr. B. Day of Snettisham.

In the section for less experienced guns, Mr. M. Duke, of Whittlesey, was first.

Hunstanton's Norfolk Gun Trading Store helped with the shoot, the first the club has held. It was staged on land owned by Thornham Farms.

▲ John Needham with his 1930s Hillman at the Fun Day in 2010.

Sports for All is the theme on the playing field with wide ranging activities from archery to tennis being played and coached during the summer.

Thornham Regatta

Thornham Regatta was a popular annual event in the late 1990s, organised by Robert Howell and the Playing Field Committee to raise funds for the old playing field.

WATER load of fun was had by visitors to Thornham harbour on Sunday when it hosted a regatta.

The activity-packed event included a raft race, stalls and a barbecue, and raised £460 for the organisers, Thornham playing field committee.

Chairman Robert Howell said: "It has been a long while since we have had a regatta in the village and we had a good turnout.

"This year was a trial run to see if there was enough interest to make the regatta an annual event and we think there was.

"Far more people came along than we had hoped for, and now we know it will be a success we can make it bigger and better next year.

"There were only four entries in the raft race but everyone involved had a lot of fun and hopefully next year we will have a few more."

The race, along the harbour, was won by a team of friends who drink in the village's Lifeboat Inn, with the playing field committee second.

Mr Howell hoped there would also be more watersports next year.

Children were also able to enter a swinner-catching competition, where they were given a line and bacon rind to catch as many swinners – a type of inedible crab – as they could. This was won by 14-year-old Jason Drewery.

Also at the regatta was a number of stalls and other sideshows.

The money raised will be used to buy new children's play equipment for the playing field.

▶ Making a splash at a Thornham regatta are (left to right) Robert Howell, Antony Needham, Robbie Wright and Mark Rix.

FAST AND FURIOUS RAFT-RACE ACTION

FULL steam ahead! Competitors in the raft race at Thornham regatta paddle furiously as they try to reach the finishing line first. The race was just one of a number of attractions at the event on Sunday, which raised £460 for the village's playing field committee.
● Full report and another picture, page 13. Picture: PETER BIRD (98/08/228A)

The Jubilee

In common with towns and villages throughout the country, Thornham celebrated the Queen's Diamond Jubilee in 2012 with a party – this one was held in the church grounds.

▶ The St. Trinian's class on Jubilee Day 1977; (left to right) Tina Johnson, Joanne Rutland, Sonja Smith, Amanda Lake, Olive Johnson (née Hart), Rodney Sutherland, and Alan Greef.

Church, Chapel & School
All Saints' Church

As well as a splendid medieval church, Thornham also had two Methodist chapels and a village school. The church dates back to the thirteenth century, the chapels and school to the nineteenth century. Only the church retains its original function, one chapel was demolished, the other is now a holiday home, as is the school.

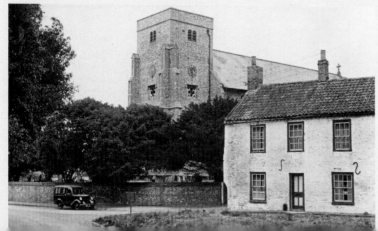

West Elevation

JANUARY.

Church of
ALL SAINTS,
THORNHAM,

MONTHLY
MAGAZINE

A·D
1897

norfolk
Link magazine

Old Hunstanton • Holme-next-the-Sea • Thornham & around the area

A complimentary FREE magazine

OCTOBER 2014

IN THIS ISSUE

MEET CHRISSY D

LOCAL EVENTS,
NOTICES & ADVERTISERS

NOTICEBOARDS

10 TIPS FOR
STARTING YOUR OWN
BUSINESS

THE COASTAL
CROPPER

GRANNY'S ATTIC
AND MORE!

www.norfolklinkmagazine.co.uk

◄ Headed 'Proposed Completion of Tower', this drawing shows a restoration in the Victorian style.

The Incorporated Church Building Society

GRANTED £40. A.D. 1903, TOWARDS RESEATING AND REPAIRING THIS CHURCH, UPON CONDITION THAT ALL THE SITTINGS ARE FOR THE FREE USE OF THE PARISHIONERS ACCORDING TO LAW.

THORNHAM BELLS TO RING OUT IN 2000

VILLAGERS in Thornham are aiming to ring in the millennium with a newly-repaired church bell.

The 1865 bell has a hole in it which has rendered it silent for many years, but it has been sent off to a specialist firm near Diss for repairs which should be completed in time to mark the arrival of 2000.

All Saints' Church has got two bells, but the small sanctus bell, believed to date back to the 13th century, has not been rung in living memory.

The church had become extremely dilapidated by the middle of the last century and a major restoration project started in the 1860s and lasted for almost 50 years.

It was during this time the bells were rehung in the tower.

Mr Henry Greef,

verger at the church for 29 years, said it was not an easy job to remove the bell from All Saints' – particularly as it poured with rain during the operation.

● RIGHT: Tony Baines gets ready to load the bell into a van after removing it from the tower for repairs. (99/08/236/8)

● BELOW: The hole which has been causing the problems. (99/08/237/11)

Pictures: ROY WILLIAMSON

Rector of Thornham moves in

THE Rev. A. C. Stewart, who was inducted to the living at Thornham on Wednesday, pictured while in the process of moving into the Rectory. (DC 4994).

DECEMBER 8, 1955.

Thornham's new Rector

THE Rev. S. Pritt, who was instituted Vicar of All Saints', Thornham, and Rector of St. Mary's, Titchwell, by the Bishop of Norwich (the Rt Rev. P. M. Herbert), on Thursday. The induction was performed by the Archdeacon of Lynn (the Ven. W. R. Musselwhite).

▲ Rev Morris Charles Russell, 1946.

▲ Margaret Rushmer and her brother, the Rev Hurrion Rushmer (rector 1927-46).

▲ Rev Geoffrey Stone, 1970.

◀ Rev Lawrence Campbell.

▲ Rev Capt Rupert Longsdale, 1965.

▲ Rev Harold C. Eves, 1951.

▲ Charles Milner, for many years a churchwarden at All Saints'.

▲ Rev Christopher Wood was a popular Rector from 2008-2013 before moving to Norwich. Christopher was regularly seen driving up and down the A149 on his scooter.

▶ Details of the medieval rood screen which dates from the fifteenth century.

◀ Rev Susan Bowden Pickstock became the first woman Rector of the Saxon Shore Benefice and All Saints' Church when she took up her post in October 2014.

Harvest Festival

The village continues the traditional Harvest Festival with a lunch in the church. Jill Bennett provides the music.

The Chapels

There were originally two Methodist Chapels on the High Street. One was demolished in the 1950s, the other was converted into a holiday home in the early part of this century.

A CENTURY ago it cost £165 1s 0d to rebuild Thornham Methodist Chapel. In comparison, structural repairs started there last week will cost about £2,000.

"It would have been as hard a task then to raise that money as it will be now to raise the £2,000" said the chapel treasurer Mr Harry Flatt.

Members of the chapel are appealing to the public for help to boost their funds. They have raised £1,000 themselves but want to put that towards decorating the interior of the building.

"So many of these little places have closed in Norfolk and throughout England and we don't want to see this one go. We want to keep it open into the next generation", said Mr Flatt.

Builders started structural repairs to the building last week and if all goes well their job should be finished by the end of September then work should start inside the building.

Chapel records do not go back further than 1870 when the building was rebuilt but Mr Flatt has a note book dating from that time showing how much money was needed for that task and how it was raised.

"It's a very interesting book that goes with a very unusual chapel — it's not often you notice one backing directly on to a church and churchyard", said Mr Flatt.

"I very much hope we will be able to raise this money. We hold two meetings each Sunday here, there is a small Sunday School and we get quite a lot of visitors too," he added.

▶ The chapel had a balcony with private seats which were hired out for two shillings a year.

The Rectory

The former Rectory was built in the nineteenth century. It is now a private home. The Drill Hall was built in the Rectory grounds in 1907.

THE VICARAGE. THORNHAM. 4.

CHURCH PAGEANT. THORNHAM 1909

The School

The School is another of the Thornham landmarks constructed by William Hogge. It was built in 1854 to cater for 140 children and closed in 1985, in spite of great efforts by the village, when numbers had dropped to twenty-six. It is now a second home.

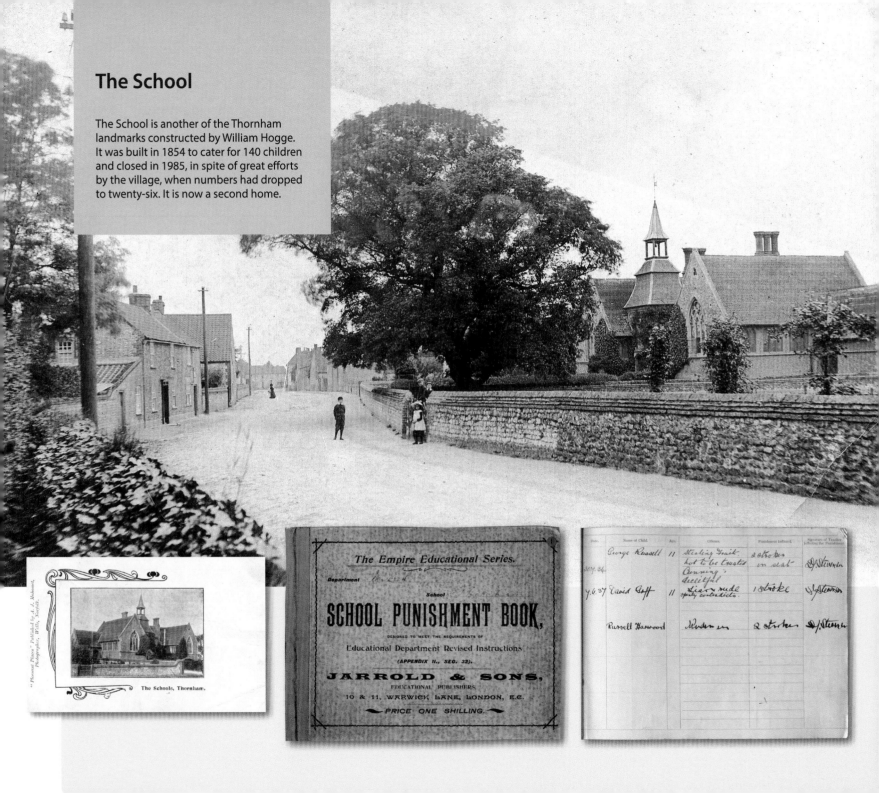

"Pleasant Places" Published by A. J. Mehonett, Photographer, Wells, Norfolk.

The Schools, Thornham.

The Empire Educational Series.

Department

School

SCHOOL PUNISHMENT BOOK,

DESIGNED TO MEET THE REQUIREMENTS OF

Educational Department Revised Instructions

(APPENDIX II., SEC. 32).

JARROLD & SONS,

EDUCATIONAL PUBLISHERS,

10 & 11, WARWICK LANE, LONDON, E.C.

— PRICE ONE SHILLING. —

Thornham School.

◀ Aubrey Sadler, Carol Deachar, Veronica Coad (née Cobb) and Maureen Crouch.

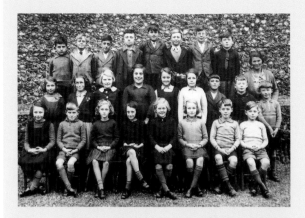

◀ The class of 1939. (left to right) Back row: George Hewitt, Bobby Bocking, Cyril Mann, Tim Siddle, Freddie Eke, Eric Green, Bruce Wilson, Neville Nudds and teacher Miss Rout.

Middle row: Peggy Cornell, Barbara Williams, Margaret Bell, Daphne Sadler, Joan Roper, Joyce Wadlow, Gerald Eke, John Bell and Trevor Williams.

Front row: Esme Ricketts (Robbie Wright's mother), Ronnie Corston, Shirley Stevenson, Ilene Ricketts, Betty Eke, Joy Matthews, Alan Sadler and Desmond Greef.

◀ Freddie Chapman, Alan Greef, Martin Steward, Charlie Groundsell, unknown, Denise Pooley, Patricia Harwood; front row: Jenny Mallett, Billy Pooley, Robert Howell, Tony Godfrey, Douglas Greef, Christine Mallett, Stephen Greef. Teacher Rose King.

▲ Dinner ladies. Back row: Beattie Hunt, Daphne Sadler and Maud Walker. Seated is Vera Goff.

▲ Back row: (left to right) Gillian Burt, Mary Rix, Shirley Riseborough, Marcia Burrell, Pamela Crown; front row: Marian Howling and Jenny Bell.

◀ Christmas 1984.

Schools plea to Whitehall

The campaign to prevent the closure of three North-West Norfolk primary schools goes to London today.

Delegations from Thornham, Ringstead and Brancaster Deepdale schools are making personal pleas to Junior Education Minister, Mr. Robert Dunn.

The meeting could decide the fate of the school at Thornham. "It will at least provide a chance for us to hammer home the crucial points," said Mrs. Ruth Wyett, a school governor.

The 130-year-old building, with its large playground and playing field, can accommodate 43 pupils, though there are at present 23 in the infant and primary classes.

The head teacher is Mrs. Jenny Jessup.

If the school were to close they would have to travel the five miles to Hunstanton — and that would mean a particularly long day for the younger pupils, said Mrs. Wyett.

While Thornham people feel their village school has the best site and facilities, making it the most suited to be retained, they are also concerned about the effect the loss of the school would have on the village.

One of the Thornham delegation will be the vicar of Old Hunstanton, the Rev. Paul Allton, who will be telling the Minister that the church is prepared to make Thornham a Church-aided school if it were the one kept open. The other delegates are Mrs. Kathy

Some of Thornham Primary School pupils with head teacher Mrs. Jenny Jessup (left) and two of the London delegation — Mr. Christopher Smith and Mrs. Ruth Wyett.

▲ After a gallant but eventually unsuccessful campaign the school was put on the market and sold as private housing.

▲ One of the last photographs of the staff and children of the School.

Weddings

A collection of weddings celebrated in the village over the past hundred years. The fashions may have changed over the years, but the sense of occasion is ever present.

▲ Tom Chambers and Alice Corston, c. 1900.

▲ Ruby Hines with her cousin 'Sonny' Middleton who gave her away in marriage to Louis Hunt, 1950s.

▲ Alfred Greef and Anna Moorhouse, 1925.

▲ Henry Greef and Joy Robson, 1952.

▲ Michael Greef and Maureen Baldwin, 1956.

▲ Nellie Tipple.

▲ Hugh Rayner and Rosemary Talbot.

▲ Tony Whiting and Ann Cock, 1960.

▲ Antony Needham and Janet Hurley, 1975.

▲ Bernard Corston & Anita Ilett, 1953.

▲ Reg Shepherd and Kathleen Southerland, 1947.

▲ Ronnie Corston and Brenda Greeves, 1954.

▲ John Lake and Shirley Riseborough, 1960.

▲ 'Spider' Goddard leads his daughter, Kara, to the church, 2009.

◀ Janet Needham with her daughter Louise, 2007.

▲ Derek Canham and Angela Southerland, 1942.

From Drill Hall to Village Hall

The Drill Hall was founded in 1907 by the Rev Nathan Waller. It was used to drill the local lads in the art of shooting. The hall served the village well as a social centre, meeting place and dance hall until 2013 when the new village hall opened.

▲ A Christmas party before the Second World War. Mr Gill of The Laurels (later Marsh Gate) is on stage as Father Christmas with his daughter Nancy, a professional ballerina. Doris Smith (née Bell), a teenager at the time recalls: 'Mr Gill financed these parties and gave a present to every child there. Oswald Waterfield from The Lifeboat Inn was the comedian, and the vicar, the Reverend Rushmer, always did recitations.'

▶ Thornham women playing darts. (left to right) Mrs Johnson, Gwen Watson, Cissy Frohawk, Aggie Potter, Mrs Arnold, Mrs Smith, Beattie Hunt, Katy Thompson, Mrs V. Helsdon and Mrs Hayter.

Opening of the Drill-Hall in the Vicarage Garden Nov. 8.

THORNHAM

Although Thornham has had the advantage of many of its near neighbours in the number of its buildings available for evening concerts and other social gatherings, it has undoubtedly outgrown in the last two or three years the accommodation afforded within the walls of its institute and schoolrooms, and the recent organisation of a local company of the Church Lads' Brigade has given further emphasis to the fact that if scope be allowed to social enterprise in the village, the necessity of finding a larger hall would at once become paramount. The vicar, the Rev. W. H. Waller, has met the difficulty by erecting in the Vicarage Grounds, at his own expense, a building capable, with the stage in position, of seating some 250 persons, and of such convenient dimensions as to afford reasonable facilities for the drill and gymnastic exercises of the Thornham Company of the C.L.B. This new Drill Hall, which is now practically completed, was, after a preliminary drill of the C.L.B., thrown open to the public at a concert given last week in aid of the funds of the C.L.B. and the Church Choir and Sunday School teachers, the musical arrangements for the occasion being placed in the hands of the Rev. F. C. Moore of Burnham Deepdale. There was no formal ceremony. The programme included several songs by Mr. Monkman (Lynn), Mr. Girley, and the Rev. F. C. Moore; pianoforte selections by Miss Elsie Moore; and a recitation by the Rev. W. H. Waller; and the entertainment, which was a thoroughly successful one, was attended by a large audience. The hall itself is a neat looking rectangular building. It is constructed on a concrete foundation, of deal match boarding covered with felt, and sheathed outside with corrugated iron. The length of the building is 55 feet, its width 25 feet, the height of the walls 10 feet, and the roof rises to some 20 feet at the ridge. The Drill Hall is fitted with movable horizontal and parallel bars, and with targets for practice with the miniature air rifle, and the arrangements are such as to allow of a range of a clear 18 yards being obtained by drawing the firing line diagonally across the building from corner to corner.

OVER £75 was raised for church expenses by a fair held in Thornham Drill Hall on Wednesday. The day long event was organised by ex-village postmistress Mrs Anna Greef. Busy serving on the fancy goods stall are Miss P. Bell, Mrs G. Sadler, Mrs N. M. Harvey and Mrs C. N. Potter. (LC 7279).

Thornham

Meeting — The annual meeting of Thornham Drill Hall committee was held at the Drill Hall. Election of officers: Mr A. E. Richmond, chairman; the Rev P. I. Allton, vice-chairman; Mr S. Hull, vice-chairman; Mrs A. Sadler, treasurer. The secretary said there was a balance of £303.48. In the Drill hall account the treasurer of the fund raising committee, Mr G. Siddle, said that a balance of £1,645.91 was in hand. The following improvements be carried out; re-wiring of the hall, remove existing stage and replace with portable stage, repair or replacement of oil-fired heating, improved entrance at south side of building, cleaning and application of sealer on floor, moving billiard table to a more convenient site within the hall.

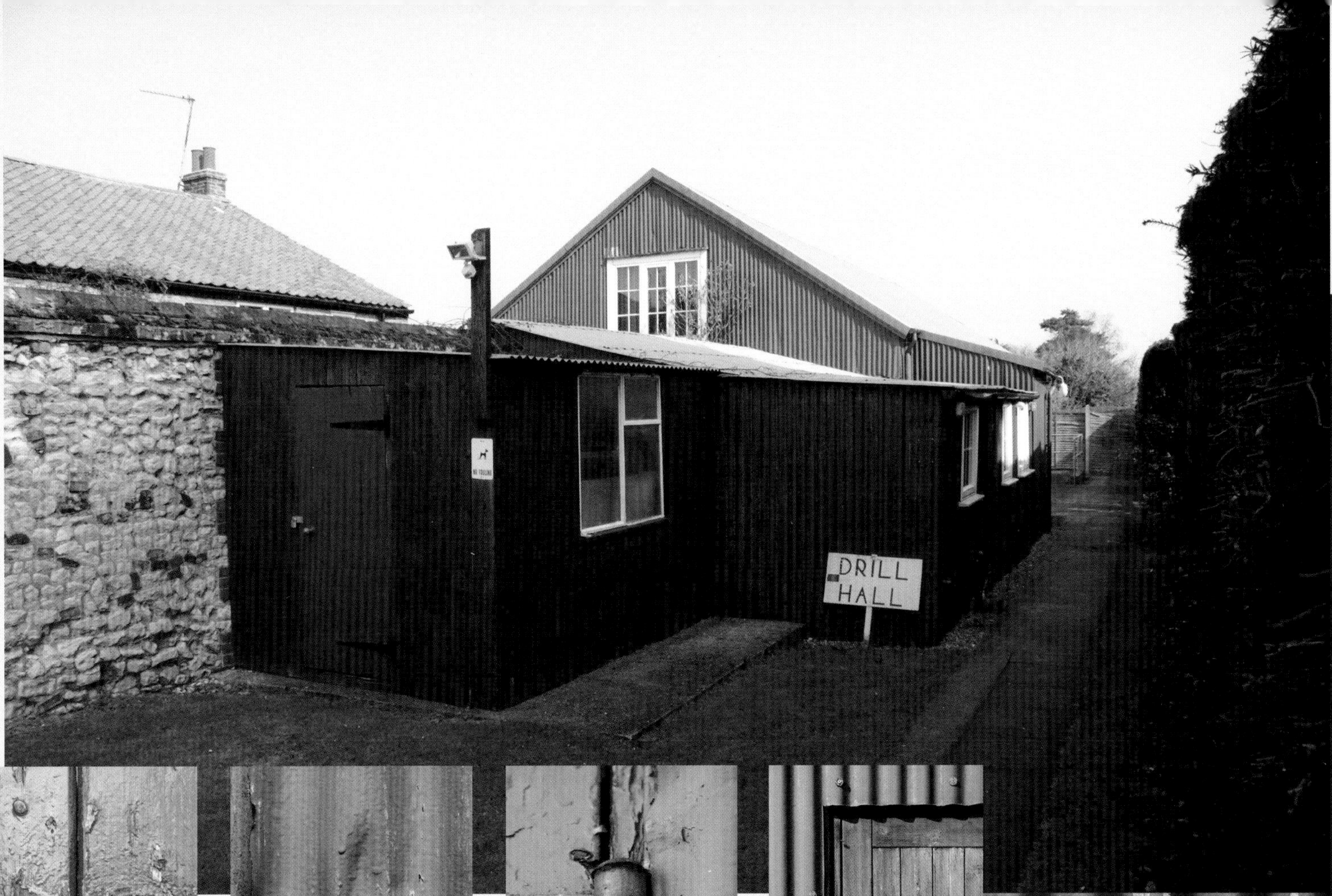
DRILL
HALL

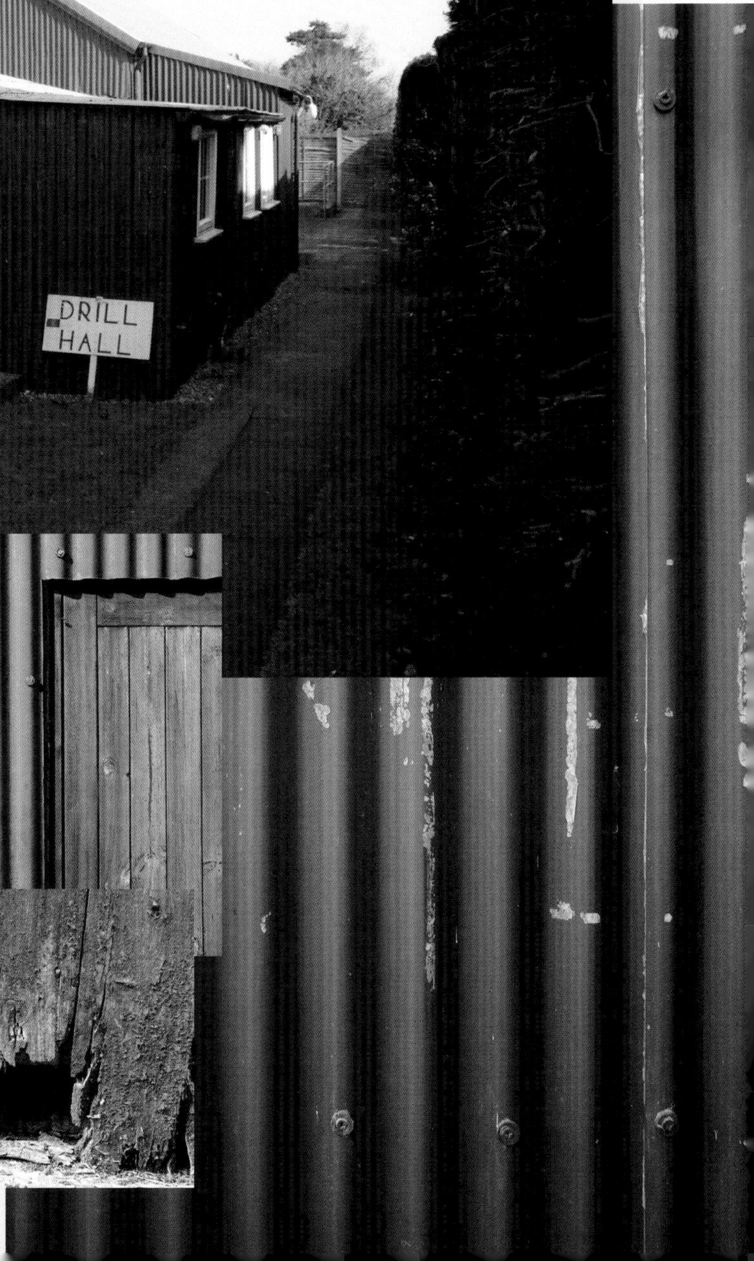

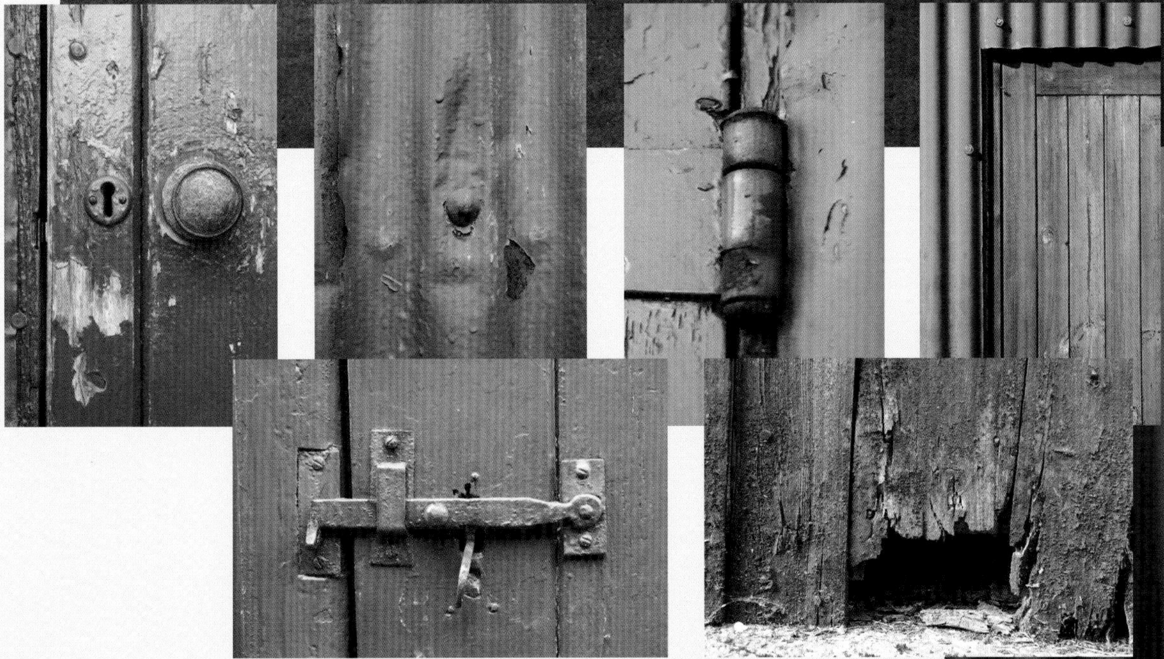

SOME MEMBERS of Thornham Youth Club go in for the more strenuous activities while others take time out to relax and chat with their friends. A number of the members travel some distance to attend meetings although the range of events is limited by space. The full-size snooker table cannot be moved out because one end of the hall has been boarded up and so dances cannot be held. (LC 8103).

POT BLACK — or simply hit the ball. It probably doesn't matter to these youth club members whether they play to the rules or not — as long as they enjoy their game.

At Thornham they certainly have all the professional gear — even if those playing are not exactly in the class of Fred Davis (LC 8103).

▲ Ralph Culley, Antony Needham, Michael Bett and Vic Hardy play the final frame of snooker in the old Drill Hall.

▲ The audience at an early performance of Thornham Village Cinema.

▶ Glenda Sadler was involved in running the Thornham Young Wives Club, Youth Club and Thornham Guild of Helping Hands and the village line dancing group, all now gone.

▲ May Craft Fair, 2013, a regular annual event in the old Drill Hall.

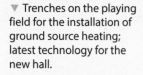

The New Village Hall

After years of fund raising and a successful grant from The National Lottery, the new village hall was built on a six acre site owned by the village, as part of a land exchange deal with local landowner, Stephen Bett. The field now has cricket and soccer pitches as well as a tennis court, a multi-use games area and a children's play area.

▶ This team of students from the CIBT Building College at Great Bircham helped to level the site.

▼ Trenches on the playing field for the installation of ground source heating; latest technology for the new hall.

New village hall 'will be for all the community'

Andrew Papworth
andrew.papworth@archant.co.uk

A topping out ceremony was held to mark the completion of Thornham's landmark new village hall and sports pavilion.

Villagers have been fundraising for a new building to replace the old Drill Hall after they gained a six-acre site for the benefit of the community.

They formed their own company, Thornham Village and Playing Field Ltd, to help bring about new facilities but quickly realised they needed to replace the dated Drill Hall, which had served the area for a century.

Having already installed a multi-use games area, they set about raising the money by selling the old site to pay for the facility.

They were then given a £475,910 Lottery grant to add to cash they had already raised in fundraising, meaning work could start on the £640,000 project earlier this year.

John Warham, chairman of Thornham Village and Playing Field Ltd, said: "The Drill Hall was about 100 years old and was really getting past its sell-by date.

"We had a fantastic site in a superb location, so it was a real opportunity to put everything together for the community."

The new building, which is due to be unveiled to the public on Saturday, September 21, once work to the inside of the building has been finished, boasts a hall which can cater for 150 people as well as a meeting room.

There are then changing rooms for the coastal village's cricket and football teams.

Mr Warham added: "We have a mixed community here. We have a lot of second home owners and caravanners, as well as people who have been here for a long time.

"This is an opportunity for people to get together and make it work for the whole community.

"We hope to involve a lot more people."

Despite the modern new building, Thornham's residents are keen not to forget the old Drill Hall which served them so well for so long.

As well as an opening ceremony for the new hall and sports pavilion in September, there will be a farewell event at the Drill Hall before villagers make their way to the new building where they will spend many hours in the future.

When the village was awarded the Lottery grant for the project last year, grant co-ordinator Colin Venes said: "It's like winning and Olympic gold medal.

"We worked hard for three years and it's a great result."

■ Site manager Steve Reeve and chairman of trustees John Warham outside the nearly completed village hall. Picture: IAN BURT

▲ New playground equipment being installed.

The Royal Opening

The hall was officially opened by HM The Queen on January 28th 2014.

Thornham Village Hall

was officially opened by

HER MAJESTY QUEEN ELIZABETH II

on 28th January 2014

Eastern Daily Press

THORNHAM VILLAGERS CELEBRATE IN STYLE

MONDAY

Court & Social

WEDNESDAY, JANUARY 29, 2014 | THE DAILY TELEGRAPH

Court Circular

SANDRINGHAM, NORFOLK
January 28th
The Queen this morning opened the new Village Hall at Thornham, Norfolk, and was received by the Chairman of Thornham Village Hall and Playing Field (Mr John Warham).

Her Majesty toured the Hall meeting Villagers, Parish Councillors and Trustees and viewing local interest activity stalls.

CLARENCE HOUSE
January 28th
The Prince of Wales and The Duchess of Cornwall this afternoon received the Canadian High Commissioner to the United Kingdom (His Excellency Mr Gordon Campbell).

His Royal Highness, Patron, Cambridge Programme for Sustainability Leadership, this evening held a Dinner at Clarence House.

The Duchess of Cornwall, President, the Brooke Hospital for Animals, this morning visited "the Brooke Through the Lens", a photographic exhibition by Richard Dunwoody, at the Gallery in the Crypt, St Martin-in-the-Fields,

Trafalgar Square, London WC2.

BUCKINGHAM PALACE
January 28th
The Duke of York this afternoon gave a Luncheon for Mr Andrew Thompson (Co-Founder and Chief Executive Officer, Proteus Digital Health) and Mr Donald Cowling (Senior Vice President) at Buckingham Palace.

BUCKINGHAM PALACE
January 28th
The Earl of Wessex, Honorary Member, this evening attended a Gala Dinner at Piz Gloria, Mürren, Switzerland, to mark the Ninetieth Anniversary of Kandahar Ski Club.

BUCKINGHAM PALACE
January 28th
The Princess Royal, Patron, Opportunity International United Kingdom, this evening held a Dinner at St James's Palace.

KENSINGTON PALACE
January 28th
The Duke of Gloucester, Vice President, Lepra, this afternoon received Ms Sarah Nancollas (Chief

◀ Eileen Richmond
and Rev Paul Irving
Allton, 1977

Heritage Exhibition

A Heritage Exhibition in 2014 revived an earlier tradition. Many of the old photos in this book emerged as a result of the Heritage Day.

Exhibition of bygones in village

"Thornham — Then and Now" is the theme for this Norfolk coastal village's tenth Spring Festival which starts today.

Relics of the village's past crafts and hobbies together with examples of today's work will make up an exhibition in All Saints' Church until Tuesday. Proceeds will go to the church fabric fund.

During the five-day festival there will also be an art exhibition in the Drill Hall, organised by well-known local artists, Marion Whittome and Robert Scott.

The church exhibition includes examples of ironwork, for which the village was famous, old photographs and other crafts.

The festival will be marked by the publication of a new booklet, "Thornham and its Story," a brief history of the village compiled by two local people, Miss P. M. A. Bett and Mr. F. S. Franklin.

The booklet traces the village's history from Roman times, recalls the legal and smuggled cargoes brought into the harbour and points the tourist towards the interesting places.

NEWS local

New soup and sandwich club proves popular

Todays Soups

TOMATO AND LENTIL

PUMPKIN

BUTTERNUT SQUASH

BROCOLLI + STILTON

LEEK + POTATO

▲ The popular soup and sandwich lunches provide an ideal meeting place throughout the winter months for friends old and new, from Thornham and surrounding villages.

Halloween Quiz Night!

Thornham Village Hall
Friday 25th October – 6.30pm
Tickets £10 each
Including Hot Supper
Bar open throughout the evening.

Book your tickets with Lou Howell:-
07831 935903
thornham.village.hall@gmail.com

FOCUS ON THORNHAM

Thornham has so much to offer you

OUT 100 years ago, the small north west Norfolk village of Thornham supported a population of 653 and some 30 shops and businesses, according to White's 1883 Directory of Norfolk.

Today, the population of the seaside village between Hunstanton and Brancaster, has fallen to around 400, but remarkably, the village is still home to more than 20 commercial concerns.

Thornham, which retains a strong agricultural element, may have lost its four 'cart owners', its three bootmakers, saddler, draper and miller from that long-ago time.

But in an era when English rural villages are facing the challenge of diminishing public transport, decreasing population and unemployment, Thornham has kept alive all its key shops and services, as well as adding a few new trades and skills.

The village still boasts a provisions' store, a bakery, traditional butcher's shop, craftsmen builders, a post office and three historic pubs, all serving Real Ale and meals.

The village garage, offering a full service to the motorist, has taken over from the wheelwright and blacksmith; other additions include a hairdresser, a firm specialising in the sale and service of lawnmowers and garden equipment, a fascinating craft centre, art gallery, German and French wine wholesaler, garden design consultant and a mushroom farm.

Thousands of visitors who come to Thornham each summer enjoy the peaceful beauty of the village, its harbour, marshes, nearby beaches and bird sanctuaries.

They fill the caravan sites, holiday homes and bed/breakfast establishments and play an important part in the village economy.

But when winter returns, the majority of shops and services rely heavily on local trade for survival — they can not exist on the income of holidaymakers alone.

In some cases, village shops can rival the big supermarkets and in addition they can offer those old-fashioned attractions of convenience, friendly service and quality merchandise.

Local shops are facilities we can not afford to lose; so next time you are in the area, shop the Thornham way and keep these businesses going another hundred years.

● A view of Thornham's picturesque church.

● There's much more to Thornham than at first meets the eye — traditional village stores run alongside more modern innovations, including a garden design consultancy. Take the time to explore its many facets next time you are in the area.

ADVERTISEMENT FEATURE

▲ A newspaper feature from 1986.

Thornham continues to have much to offer to both residents and visitors alike. Quiz nights, Zumba and Christmas parties are regular events.

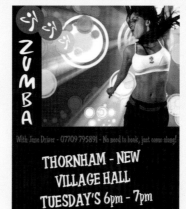

ZUMBA

With Jane Driver - 07709 795891 - No need to book, just come along!

THORNHAM - NEW VILLAGE HALL TUESDAY'S 6pm - 7pm

Come join the party and shake those calories away!

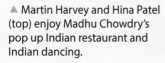

▲ Martin Harvey and Hina Patel (top) enjoy Madhu Chowdry's pop up Indian restaurant and Indian dancing.

Children's events, art exhibitions, table-top sales, cinema and theatre evenings are all part of the fabric of village life in the new hall.

Street Scenes
The Village Sign

The much photographed Village Sign was first unveiled by Eileen Richmond. It was restored and repainted in 2013. Vic Hardy and Antony Needham are seen here on two separate occasions, reinstalling the sign.

Iron trade recalled in village sign

THORNHAM'S once-famous ironworks is the major feature on the new village sign, which was unveiled on Stocks Hill last Saturday.

Presented by Thornham Thursday Club, the sign has been designed and made by Mr P. J. Hillard of South Wootton, who was among the crowd watching the unveiling ceremony.

Performing the honours were Mrs Eileen Richmond, founder-chairman of the club, and 94-year-old Mrs Mary Goold, its oldest member. The sign was dedicated by the vicar, the Rev Paul Allton.

On one side of the sign, two men are shown working in Thornham ironwork's foundry. The scene is taken from the original sign at the ironworks, with background added, said Mrs Richmond.

She pointed out that King Edward VII was very interested in the ironworks, and the ornate gates leading to the kitchen gardens at Sandringham House had been made there.

The wrought iron workers also fared well at major exhibitions. They took the gold medal in Brussels in 1910 and the bronze medal in Paris in 1900.

Above the ironworks is a representation of the old church. To the sides are the Roman burial urn, which was found nearby, and a bishop's mitre, to symbolise the name for Thornham in the Doomesday Book — Bishop's Tornham.

The shield below shows the red ensign and bell of HMS Thornham, which was named after the village.

On the other side of the sign, the main feature is the

village's former windmill, a granary, a coal barn and the Jessie Mary, the last trading vessel to use the harbour.

Above this is the present-day church and below, the Thursday Club shield. To the sides are trees, as a reminder that the area was once all woodland, and a seabank, to represent the Dutchman Van Haesdoncke's work on the sea defences.

The sign is set in a plinth built by Mr Tim Siddle of Thornham flints donated by Mr H. Bett.

On behalf of the parish council, chairman Mr R. Baker accepted the sign.

He said it had been put in a most appropriate position as the green contained the chestnut tree planted to commemorate Queen Victoria's diamond jubilee, and was also the site of the village stocks.

The ceremony concluded with refreshments at All Saints' Church.

◀ The sign shows the Thornham Ironworks on one side and the harbour, Granary, Coal Barn and Mill on the reverse.

The East End

The east end of the village photographed in the late nineteenth century, with Jones' pit, now overgrown and fenced in. In the background is Malt House Farm. The house looks much the same now as it did then, but the outbuildings have been converted into houses.

THORNHAM — EAST

The former Men's Institute, now renamed Copper Hall, (just behind the horse chestnut tree) was run by Norman Raven. Darts and snooker were played there. In the years before 1850 the building was used as a school.

◄ Copper Hall in 1967 and (above) in 2014.

Formerly Vic Helsden's Dairy Farm House before becoming home to Robert and Marion Montgomery. Now a second home.

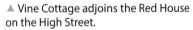

▲ Vine Cottage adjoins the Red House on the High Street.

▶ West End Cottages – in common with many of the old cottages in the village, they were built at right angles to the main road.

▲ Primrose Cottage. The home of Aggie Potter and later, Marjorie Webster, before becoming a second home. Sadly, the front door is no longer painted primrose.

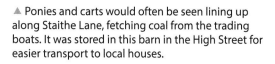

Ponies and carts would often be seen lining up along Staithe Lane, fetching coal from the trading boats. It was stored in this barn in the High Street for easier transport to local houses.

▲ Family group sitting outside Red Brick House. The caption on the back has the cryptic comment, 'Isn't it a shame I have cut off Mrs Gray'.

◄ Agnes Raven, formerly Larter, née Hines, sometime housekeeper and resident at Red Brick House, when it was owned by the Raven family.

4374. Hall Lane, Thornham

THORNHAM. NORFOLK.

Views taken from the church tower, looking up Hall Lane. The photo on the right is from 2006.

For many years, brothers Bill and Ben Howard lived in this cottage at the bottom of Church Street. They were known to enjoy a pint and a singsong in The Lifeboat.

Bill and Ben's Cottage

Church Cottage at Thornham.

THE LOCALS know Church Cottage, Thornham, as 'Bill and Ben's cottage'.

It goes back to the days when two elderly brothers lived in the house but never spoke to each other and even walked along different lanes to get to the village pub.

Originally a pair of fishermen's cottages dating back to 1628, it was reconstructed in the early 17th century. Although it has been converted into a single dwelling, there are still two staircases so it would be relatively easy to turn it back to two homes again.

Traditionally built of colour-washed chalk, brick and flint, it has been modernised but still retains the warmth and character of its early days with its exposed beams, latch doors and inglenook fireplace.

It is one of the most attractive cottages in the village and overlooks farmland towards the harbour, salt marshes and nature reserve, and most of the rooms have splendid views.

The inglenook is in the sitting room and there is another brick fireplace with woodburner in the open plan dining room/kitchen which has pine units and access to the sunken patio area and the garden.

There is also a study on the ground floor and upstairs there is a main bedroom with en suite bathroom, two further bedrooms and a shower room.

Facing Church Street and overlooking open meadows, it has an enclosed garden of about a quarter of an acre, with outbuildings and parking space.

The agents, Beltons Country Homes and Cottages, say that planning consent could be approved for an extension to be built with two bedrooms, a bathroom, conservatory, utility room and cloakroom.

The property is on the market for a figure in the region of £175,000.

LEFT: Inside Church Cottage at Thornham.

▲ Ben Howard.   ▲ Bill Howard.

▲ The cottage adjoining All Saints' Church has been much transformed since this early 1980s photograph (top).

Church Street, Thornham

CRAFTSMEN
DEREK BATTERBEE
HARRY BIRD
MICHAEL GODDARD
VIC HARDY
ROBERT HOWELL
JAKE JOHN
ANTONY NEEDHAM
JOHN NEEDHAM
PETER OLIVER
ARCHITECTS
FRANK BRADBEER
ANN DIETRICH

▲ The bus shelter at the top of Church Street was built by the villagers to celebrate the Millennium. It is a regular stopping place for the popular Coasthopper bus service.

▶ The bus shelter was built by local craftsmen, including (left to right) Robert Howell, designer Frank Bradbeer, Antony Needham and Mark Rix. The plaque lists all those involved.

The gates to the Manor House can be seen in these two photographs of Church Street. The former village shop is on the left hand side of the picture.

CHURCH STREET

CHURCH STREET THORNHAM

Church Street Thornham.

The Manor

The origins of Thornham Manor go back to the early sixteenth century but, in spite of its vaguely Tudor appearance, the current house only dates from 1904, built by Major Oswald Ames. The Manor was split into three separate properties in 2005.

▲ The Manor at the time of its rebuilding in the early 1900s.

▲ The Manor today, renovated and divided into three.

◀ Major Oswald Ames sent this Christmas card to his gardener Alfred Greef.

Wishing you both a merry Xmas & Happy New Year. O.H.A.

▲ A postcard from 1920.

▲ Construction of The Manor gardens.

3215. MANOR HOUSE

▲ Henry, Desmond and Michael Greef, 1939.

▼ Lord Fermoy at a garden opening ceremony.

MANOR HOUSE THORNHAM.

▲ The formal garden today.

◄ There is a little-noticed relief of Queen Victoria built into the outside wall surrounding the Manor.

◄ Aerial view of The Manor following its division and development.

The Hall

Thornham Hall was built by George Hogge in the middle of the eighteenth century. Hogge was a successful King's Lynn businessman who owned some thirty trading ships as well as the building in Tuesday Market Place which became Barclays Bank and is now Fraser Dawbarns, Solicitors. Hogge was also co-owner of the Hogge & Seppings Brewery at Setch, suppliers of beer to The Lifeboat Inn.

▲ The Hall as drawn for a 1778 planning map.

▶ Henry Bett with Stephen and Charles.

This hall may be pulled down JAN. 1955

◀ The Hall was let out to tenant farmers for seventy years until 1953. During this time the Archdale/Hogge families lived in The Cottage on High Street. When Henry Bett moved into the Hall in the 1950s, it was full of damp and dry rot and came close to being demolished.

▲ Margaret Bett, mother of Stephen and Charles.

▲ Charles Bett and family.

▲ Stephen Bett.

▲ The Hall and its park in the foreground.

The Red House

The Red House, another of George Hogge's buildings, has been lived in by descendants of the Hogge/Archdale family since it was built. When the new main Coast Road was built (the old one wound down Staithe Lane past the Lifeboat and around the Green) it cut through the gardens of the Red House, which still occupy both sides of the road.

▲ Arriving at the Red House.

▲ Mrs Edith Ames Lyde (1850-1914), Thornham's Lady of the Manor (left), outside The Red House with Mrs Evelyn Grange, Eileen Richmond's mother. The Grange Family lived in the house in the years before the First World War.

▶ Edith Eliza, daughter of William Samuel Hogge married Lionel Ames in 1873.

Thornham Red Cross Voluntary Aid Detachment.

◀ Two of Thornham's Red Cross nurses, Posy and Barbara Villiers.

The Voluntary Aid Detachment system was started in 1909 and Mrs Ames Lyde formed a group in Thornham. The VAD nurses staffed the Red House during the First World War when it was used as an auxiliary hospital for wounded soldiers.

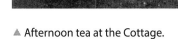
THORNHAM COTTAGE

The Cottage

The Cottage, home to Edith and Lionel Ames Lyde, and where Henry and Pleasance Bett were brought up. It is now the home of Joe Davies and Peter Gold.

▲ Afternoon tea at the Cottage.

◄ The Cottage is one of the oldest houses in the village, the date is on the porch.

In the 1970s it was sold and divided into two homes, but has now been restored as one building.

▲ Queen Alexandra, Edith Ames Lyde and Victor Ames at The Cottage for the royal inspection of Thornham's British Red Cross nurses in 1911. There was a display of first aid techniques.

Drove House

Drove House ws built in 1710 and was originally the Rectory for the parishes of Thornham and Holme. The Jamieson family first came to Drove House in 1910. Drove Orchards was started by David Jamieson in 1952. His son Andrew now runs the expanded Drove Farm Orchards site.

PROGRAMME

DROVE HOUSE,
THORNHAM

GYMKHANA

AND

SPORTS

FRIDAY, AUGUST 31st, 1934
commencing at 2.15 p.m.

◀ Major David Jamieson (seen here in later years with his batman Harry Flatt,) won the Victoria Cross while leading his men in an almost suicidal defence of the Orne Bridgehead soon after the D-Day landings. The medal, he always said, was won by his men. Brenda Flatt, one of Harry Flatt's daughters, still lives in the village.

Coastguard Cottages

These pictures show Coastguard Cottages in a different age, when sheep and cows were grazed on The Green in line with common grazing rights dating back to the Enclosure Acts of the eighteenth century.

THE GREEN, THORNHAM. J 7729. (Moorhouse's Series.)

3212. THE GREEN & COASTGUARD STATION, THORNHAM.

▲ Coastguard Cottages with the pond known as Monty's Pit, named after Monty Bell who lived close by.

Reed cutting on the marsh takes place every year in February and March. Billy Temple (left, in green) has been cutting the reeds on Thornham marsh for nearly forty years. Richard Matthews (right) from West Runton is pictured here bundling the reeds.

Coast Guard Cottage has been owned by well-known local artist, Shirley (Carnt) Deterding, for more than fifty years and has stunning views over the marshes. Shirley uses the cottage as her studio. When the Deterdings moved here more than fifty years ago, it was little more than a simple 'two up, two down' dwelling.

At work in her studio;

The Enclosure Acts of the 1790s finally determined the rights of villagers regarding the enclosure of traditional common, grazing and parish lands. These rights have carried forward 225 years and remain in place today. The Green is owned by the Cattle Gate Holders, via forty-nine 'stints' or shares; forty-six of which are owned by the Bett family, two by the Parish Council and one by Margaret Bunkle.

The caption to this 1911 photograph says: 'Hughes Hovel'. In times of hardship and homelessness, people did build their own 'hovel' homes. Perhaps Hughes was a man down on his luck.

◀ The Green, looking east across the pond known mysteriously as the *Queen of Sheba*.

◀ Reg. Baker's house on The Green, then and (below left) now.

GREEN LANE, THORNHAM.

▲ Green Lane looking towards Herga Cottage before the council houses were built.

Flooding does happen, though in these cases, caused by run-off from the land, not from the sea.

▲ Ivy Needham and son Antony survey the scene outside Trees Cottage.

◀ Antony Needham's wife Janet inspects the water levels outside The Chapel many years later, with Lucinda Reddyhoff.

Scaffolding

There has hardly been a month over the past ten years, when renovation, conversion or new building has not been taking place in the village. These pictures show some examples.

◀ Staithe Lane at high tide.

Getting about …

Over the years, residents have used a variety of
transport for getting about, and have had to
negotiate everyting from high tides on Staithe Lane
to winters when they were snowed in.

▲ January 1987.

◀ It takes more than a fall of snow
to keep Neville Nudds off his bike.

▶ Tony Whiting.

▲ This Westland helicopter landed on the old Playing Field in 1962 as part of army manoeuvres on the marsh.

▲ Flying in for lunch – this helicopter brought a guest to the Orange Tree to celebrate his 80th birthday.

▼ The popular Coasthopper bus provides an essential mode of transport for residents and visitors alike. It is particularly busy during the summer months.

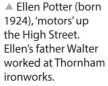

▲ Ellen Potter (born 1924), 'motors' up the High Street. Ellen's father Walter worked at Thornham ironworks.

◀ Bald tyres were OK in 1929.

◀ A special occasion.

Villagers

In common with many rural communities, the social and economic structure of the village has undergone vast changes over the past 100 years or so. In the middle of the nineteenth century, Thornham had a population of 1500 most of whom worked on the land, with village crafts and trades providing virtual self sufficiency. Today the population is less than 500 and half of the houses are second homes.

The following pages reflect these changes and show a cross section of the villagers over the years.

Lynn News & Advertiser, Tuesday, Augu.. 18, 1970. 5

PICTURESQUE THORNHAM: SPOTLIGHT ON SOME OF ITS FRIENDLY PEOPLE

By Carolyn Watts

KING'S HEAD Hotel sign is a striking example of Thornham iron work. (KC 2812).

LLS AND TOYS that were the treasures of great-grandmothers find a good home with Mrs. A. Greef. (KC 2822).

THORNHAM is one of the most picturesque villages on the North Norfolk coast and one that has taken its history by the hand and led it firmly into the 20th century. Trippers driving along the coast road from Old Hunstanton may pass through Thornham taking it for granted that the pretty home-stone or whitewashed cottages crouched around the church belong to the affluent "weekenders" who abound around this stretch of coast.

Not so. There are only 30 of these part-time residents in Thornham and even they are enough to worry the postman, Henry Greef.

For 19 years he has cycled round with the village letters and parcels but next year the mail for Thornham will be motorised from Hunstanton and Mr. Greef takes over as Thornham's postmaster.

As he said, "It's a bit of a job finding some of these week-enders nobody knows, I'm not sure chaps in vans will find it easy at all."

45 years

At present Thornham post office is run by Mr. Greef's mother who came to the village 45 years ago as Miss Moorehouse to open a fancy goods shop.

Since then she has been married, had three sons and been widowed but the shop carries on in the best tradition of village shops.

Prayer books, buckets and spades, birthday cards and babies' dresses mingle happily with official notices about pensions and licences.

But the most interesting thing about Mrs. Greef is something not everybody knows, although the Royal family know.

At the back of her house she has converted a fine old barn and its hay-loft into what must be one of the biggest private collections of Victorian toys in existence.

Royal visits

vast amount of beer the floor was left simmering in (fine beer, he recalls, brewed by Hogg and Seppings of Setch) who delivered by cart and horse and allowed their men to stay the night if the journey back was too much to accomplish the same day's.

Smugglers

Smugglers, of course, there were but Mr. Waterfield holds that they used a row of cottages that stood opposite—and whose foundations he has seen turned up by the plough this year.

His mother often told the tale of an old gentleman who was not averse to storing tobacco, hot from the runners hands, in his loft.

"The Excise men were suspicious so they called early one morning. 'My loft's wide open you can search it' he said. They didn't bother after that and searched his rooms but found nothing, so off they went. Of course his loft was piled high with tobacco which he used to take to Wisbech on a horse-drawn cart, covered with coal," says Mr. Waterfield.

But times changed and on the wall of the Lifeboat is a sad picture of the "Jessie Marie" in full sail, the last boat to leave Thornham harbour.

The Lifeboat fell on hard times, until holiday makers discovered its great stretches of sand that are still rather inaccessible. Back came the trade as the Lifeboat was back in trade.

Its bars have their own

charm, a cosy lounge lit by the glow of oil lamps, a bigger one with the air of a Scottish baronial hall and the public bar wherein is found the ancient game of "Penny in the Hole".

Thirteen pennies should be thrown at a hole in a wooden bench under which is a drawer. Players throw in turns to see who can get all the pennies in first and if anyone gets all 13 in with one turn the landlord presents them with a bottle of whisky.

This has only happened once in Mr. Waterfield's time.

Bar skittles

Another traditional bar room game is played at The Chequers — skittles. After only two months the new landlord, Mr. Richard Sidey, has become a dab hand with the wooden ball that is swung in circles at the pins.

Mr. Sidey and his wife Dorothy are newcomers to the licensed trade as well as to Thornham but so far they like both and hope to see the Chequers become popular with the "locals" as well as the visitors.

Dominating the little triangle that is the village green is All Saints Church, rising from a veil of trees.

Inside, it is light and airy, no stained glass windows, and has a simplicity that is peaceful.

A closer inspection shows carved pew heads featuring a series of men being swallowed by a monster.

There is so much to see in Thornham, if only you know where to look — and if you do not know ask the people who live there. They are very friendly.

'WE'RE CHEATING a bit really," says Mr. W. E. Walker (RIGHT) when asked about the fine old Thornham Iron Workers' sign that hangs outside his filling station and garage.

The original workers designed and made wrought iron pieces that were famous but they closed down in about 1913 when their benefactress died.

"As we are the only people in the village who do any iron work now, we thought we would give the sign a home," Mr. Walker told us. (KC 2819).

CARS ON the coast road pass through the centre of Thornham where many holiday makers stop to admire the charming picture of the King's Head Hotel with its roses round the door, the village green and the church. (KC 2820).

▲ A newspaper feature from 1970.

▲ Ian Barrett.

▲ Nick Mocatta.

▲ Terry Morris.

▲ Patrick Ballanger.

▲ John Woods, a Thornham shell-fisherman and owner of the *Abby Onar*. He's thought to have been the father (or possibly uncle) of Nathaniel Woods, master of the *Jessie Mary*. At the time of the 1901 census he was sixty-eight, married to Eleanor and lived in one of the cottages on the south side of The Green.

▼ Duncan Bolt hosted meetings of the International Society of Knot Tyers at his home in Eaton Cottage.

▼ Des Pawson MBE is pictured (right) showing how it should be done. Des has written many books on knot tying and runs a successful business Footrope Knots.

The 'Bight' 1913. Self.

▲ Violet (née Napier) Ames with her camera on Thornham beach in 1913. Several of the photographs in this book, covering the period 1910 to 1930, were taken by her. She and her husband Victor Ames built Marshlands, and her brother Oswald built Thornham Manor.

The Ames albums, three volumes of family photographs, can be seen in the Norwich Millennium Library.

▲ Victor Ames designed metalwork for Thornham Ironworks.

▲ Victor Ames outside Ivy Cottage.

▶ The Archdale children in the 1890s.

▼ Pleasance Bett with her brother Henry and their parents, Margaret (née Archdale) and Stafford Henry Imlach Bett.

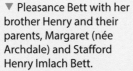

▲ Pleasance Bett and Joan Ames on Thornham beach in the 1920s.

▲ The Ames children, Joan and Maurice (standing), father Victor in the back, with Alfred Cobb at the rear wheel.

◀ Alfred Cobb, gardener at Marshlands, gives a ride in a home-made punt to Joan and Maurice Ames, as their father, Victor, looks on.

▲ Pleasance Bett.

◄ Evelyn Grange is seated extreme left; second from right, standing, is Mary Ann Asker.

► Eileen Richmond (right) seen here in her pre-war nursing days. In 1939 Eileen married RAF pilot John Humphreys. Tragically, he was killed in a plane crash on the eve of their first wedding anniversary. Eileen became a Land Army girl during the war and later married Arthur 'Ricky' Richmond, who ran one of Thornham's mushroom farms.

◄ Clifford Grange outside The Red House. Clifford and his wife Evelyn were Eileen Richmond's parents.

◄ Bryony Richmond and her father, Ricky.

► Henry and Doris Cobb on their wedding day in 1939. The bungalow, called Hendor, which Henry built, was demolished in 2014.

◄ Ernest and Eliza (Dolly) Grange and their granddaugher, Eileen (later Richmond). The Grange Family lived in The Red House for a while.

◀ Henry Cobb and Ian Hopper.

▲ Doris Cobb.

◀ Veronica Coad (née Cobb) with her father, Henry, arriving at the Church, 1966.

▶ Vic and Sue Hardy ran the village garage. Vic keeps the Thornham ironworking tradition going while Sue balances the books for both the Village Hall and the Church.

▲ David Thompson driving one of the International Harvesters tractors which he lovingly restores.

▲ Ben Howard (brother to Bill), Tom Frohawk and Albert Walker all spent their working lives on the land. Albert, who was married to Millie (née Groundsell), was at Ling Farm for many years. He and Millie had two children, Luan (Llewellyn) and Vera.

▶ Monica Clare and Ben Howard in the 1970s.

William Ducker (top left), Thornham shopkeeper, with members of the Thornham Brotherhood on an excursion with his wagon. The Brotherhood was a local branch of a national nineteenth/early twentieth-century men's association. Among those also believed to be in the photograph are coal merchant Frank Callaby, Amos Sutherland, George Howard, James Rason, Reuben Eagle and Charles and Matthew Middleton.

THE THORNHAM BROTHERHOOD

◀ Billy Ducker.

▶ The Burt family are long term village residents. Andy has taken an active part in the sporting life of Thornham.

▲ Brothers John and Antony Needham.

▲ Martin Goodsell is one of a number of artists in Thornham.

▲ Melanie Venes at work on her loom. Melanie is an expert weaver.

▲ Clive Wakes-Miller is passionate about his bees.

▲ Eric Beck in 1942 before going to the Far East with the Royal Norfolks.

▲ The wedding of Eric Beck to Rene Woods, 1949.

◀ Ruby Beck, sister of Eric.

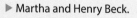

▶ Martha and Henry Beck.

▲ Hina Patel trying to get a tune out of the old piano.

▲ Alastair Symington, current Chairman of the Playing Field Committee.

▲ Shirley Lake.

▲ Peter Oliver, author of the book *Thornham – a Photographic Portrait of a Norfolk Village*.

▲ Thomas Edwardes Southerland.

▲ Ralph Culley is Chairman of Thornham soccer and cricket teams.

◀ Luke Auker was a longshore fisherman. This rare photograph is a glass ambrotype and probably dates from the 1850s.

160

▲ Monica Clare with Caroline Bartram.

▲ Odile Castro.

◀ Celia Hardiment and Eva Riseborough.

▲ Harriet Proudfoot married Stephen Hewitt, who was a gardener at The Manor. They lived in Eaton Cottage and had three sons, George, Sam and Harry.

▶ Maurice Chapman, farm manager for Henry Bett, lived at Thornham Ling.

▲ Alison Corby.

▲ Sheila Redman.

▲ Peter Goff.

▲ Barry and Jenny Langford.

▲ 'Spider' and Margaret Goddard.

▲ Kara Goddard.

▲ Ronnie, Annie and Nathaniel Corston.

▲ Noah Francis, Thornham ironworker, with (top) his wife and the rose he made.

▲ Helen and Steve Stafford.

▲ Jimmy Goddard runs a successful gardening business in the area.

◀ Sam Proudfoot in his Church Lads' Brigade uniform. He was killed in the First World War.

▶ Harold Mann lived at Thornham Ling, where he worked on the farm.

▲ Olive Johnson (née Hart), holding the pony.

Aggie Potter.

▲ Ellen Howell (née Potter) and Gwen Watson in their Red Cross Uniforms. Many Thornham girls joined the Thornham Red Cross, then organised by Mrs Bett to provide first aid training. Ellen says: 'I still hadn't earned my red cross when this picture was taken.'

▲ Jane Bridges, Ellen Howell's grandmother, standing outside Primrose Cottage. This house was also home to Aunt Aggie, a keen gardener and regular at the Chelsea Flower Show. She loved wild primroses and painted her front door the colour of the flowers.

▶ Harriet Skeet, grandmother of Ellen Howell and great-grandmother to Robert (Holly), Leslie and Barbara Howell, and great-great grandmother to Beverley and Louise Howell.

▲ Robert, Carole and Louise Howell.

▲ Vincent's 100th birthday.

▶ Vincent Sadler and Bessie Playford.

▶ Vincent in the field behind The Lifeboat.

▶ Tom, Lizzie and Cedric Sadler.

▲ Vincent Sadler was the local baker. He emigrated to Canada as a young man before returning to Thornham and living to the ripe old age of 101. The Sadler family ran The Lifeboat Inn for many years.

▲ Robert and Mary Ann Asker.

◀ Mrs Parnell (with dog) chatting to Ruby Beck outside The Lifeboat Inn.

◀ Herbert John Bunkle and Jane Elizabeth Asker on their wedding day, 1900.

▶ Mrs Parnell's house was behind the pub.

▲ Belinda Hamer.

▲ Mabel Howes.

▲ Gillian Rix.

▲ John and Mary Greef with their children. The youngest here is Alfred, who started the Thornham Greef dynasty. He arrived in the village in 1905 to work for Oswald Ames as a gardener at Thornham Manor.

▶ Alfred Greef was wounded at Delville Wood on the Somme in 1916.

◀ Stephen Greef.

▲ Samuel and Sarah Jones.

▼ Colvy Jones.

▼ Daphne Siddle.

▲ George Hines, a Chief Petty Officer in submarines, was awarded the Distinguished Service Medal. After the war he was a familiar figure in The Lifeboat with his dog Sadie.

▲ Ruby Hines.

▲ John Abraham Davis's father ran the King's Head pub in the 1850s. John married Mary Ann Sampson in Thornham church in 1864. They lived on Oldfield Green where John worked as an agricultural labourer before moving to The Cottage and then to Church Street.

▶ May Butters.

▲ George Seapey, one of the last lime-kiln workers. The lime kilns were at the top of Ringstead Road.

▲ William Seapey.

▲ Kathleen Southerland.

▲ Joy Matthews.

First Published 2015.

© Text and modern photographs copyright John Warham 2015. Archive photographs are the copyright of their respective owners and are reproduced with permission. All rights reserved. No part of this publication may be reproduced or stored in a retrieval system or transmitted in any form or by any means, electronic, mechanical, photocopying or otherwise without the prior written permission of the publisher.

The right of John Warham to be identified as the author of this work has been asserted in accordance with the Copyright, Designs and Patents Act 1988.

ISBN 978-0-9553333-7-8

A catalogue record for this book is available from the British Library.

Designed by Dick Malt

Published by Thornham Local History Society
Red Brick House, Hall Lane
Thornham, Norfolk PE36 6NB

Printed in Norfolk by Swallowtail Print
www.swallowtailprint.co.uk

Acknowledgements

This book could not have been produced without the help of so many local families and other contributors. They include, in alphabetical order, the following:

Lynette Bailey, Eric Beck, Michael Bett, Stephen Bett, David & Wendy Brooks, Adrian Brown, Monica Clare, Veronica Coad, Ronnie & Brenda Corston, Michael Corston, Yvonne Fleming, Daniel Gibson, 'Spider' & Margaret Goddard, Mark Goode, Malcolm Greenwood, John Giles, Vic & Sue Hardy, Ian Heighton of the King's Morris, Jacqueline Johnson, Neil Holmes, Robert & Carole Howell, John & Shirley Lake, Malcome Larter, Cyril Mann, the late Bob le Masurier, Mike McDonnell, Charles Milner, Helen Millin, Stephanie Mocatta, Vernon Maldoom, Chris Neal, Antony & Janet Needham, John Needham, Charles & Vicky Rangeley-Wilson, the late Ted Rason, Jacqueline Roberts, Mary Rutland, Mandy Sadler, Adrian Siddle, Doris Smith, Helen Stafford, Emma Tagg, Annelli Taylor, David & Pat Thompson, Janie Thompson, Jo Toop, Alison Wakes-Miller, Tony & Ann Whiting, Jeanne Whittome, Ron Williamson, Arthur & Jean Wilson, Tom & Sylvia Webb, and Mark & Ruth Wyett.

In addition we would like to acknowledge the following: The Norwich Millennium Library, the Norfolk Record Office, Gressenhall Rural Life Museum and the Wisbech & Fenland Museum. We also thank Eric Secker and *KL Magazine*, Archant and *Lynn News* for permission to reprint some of their photographs and for the use of some archive material.

Special thanks to Julia Rafferty for use of the photos of HM The Queen's visit; Graham Dennis, formerly of Johnson's Row, and to Mary Rutland and Mandy Sadler for allowing us to use their personal scrapbook collections, and to Peter Oliver for allowing me generous use of his text from the book, *Thornham – A Photographic History of a Norfolk Village*.

Every reasonable effort has been made to establish and contact the copyright holders of all the photographs used in this book. Any errors or omissions are inadvertent and anyone who has not been contacted is invited to write to the publisher so that a proper acknowledgement can be included in any subsequent editions of this book.

Bibliography

Thornham – A Photographic Portrait of a Norfolk Village – Peter Oliver, Pat Thompson & John Warham 2006

Thornham – People and Places – John Warham 2009

The Lawless Coast – Neil Holmes 2008

Kelly's and White's *Directories*

Behind the View – Elizabeth Handy

A Dream of the land – John Hansell

East Anglia – Hammond Innes

East Anglia Villages – John Potter

East Anglia Panoramas – John Potter

Norfolk at Work - Neil Storey

Norfolk Fowler – Alan Savory

English Villages – Life in the Countryside – Valerie Porter

Thornham and its Story – PMA Bett & FS Franklin 1974, revised Charles Milner 2004

All Saints' Church, Thornham – T Hugh Bryant

John Warham has lived in Thornham since 2000. He has produced a series of four photographic books on villages of the North Norfolk Coast, entitled *People and Places*. He also worked with Peter Oliver and Pat Thompson on *Thornham – A Photographic History*.

Stephen Greef was born and brought up in Thornham where he attended the village school. Stephen is proud of his village roots and has never lost contact with Thornham. He and his wife Megan moved back to the village in 2013.

Dick Malt has designed all of the books in the People & Places series.